D1588132

Budapest

World Cities series

Edited by
Professor R.J. Johnston and Professor P. Knox

Published titles in the series:

Mexico City *Peter Ward*
Lagos *Margaret Peil*
Tokyo *Roman Cybriwsky*
Budapest *György Enyedi and Viktória Szirmai*
Hong Kong *C.P. Lo*

Forthcoming titles in the series:

Paris *Daniel Noin and Paul White*
Rome *John Agnew and Calogero Muscarà*
Lisbon *Jorge Gaspar and Allan Williams*
New York City *David Johnson and Eugenie L. Birch*
Vienna *Elisabeth Lichtenberger*
Melbourne *Kevin O'Connor*
Warsaw *Joanna Regulska and Adam Kowalewski*
Taipei *Roger M. Selya*
Calcutta *Ramendra De*
Seoul *Joochul Kim and Sang-Chual Choi*
Dublin *Andrew MacLaren*
Brussels *Alexander B. Murphy*
Randstad *Frans M. Dieleman, Rein B. Jobse and Jan van Weesep*
Montreal *Annick Germain and Damaris Rose*
Birmingham *Gordon Cherry*

Other titles in preparation

Budapest

A Central European Capital

Györgi Enyedi and
Viktória Szirmai

English translation by Vera Gáthy
English translation revised by Charles Hebbert

Belhaven Press
London
Co-published in the Americas by Halsted Press,
an imprint of John Wiley & Sons, Inc., New York

© György Enyedi and Viktória Szirmai, 1992

First published in Great Britain in 1992 by
Belhaven Press (a division of Pinter Publishers Limited)
25 Floral Street, London WC2E 9DS

All rights reserved. No part of this publication may be reproduced,
stored in a retrieval system, or transmitted by any other means
without the prior permission of the copyright holder. Please direct
all enquiries to the publishers.

*Co-published in the Americas by Halsted Press, an imprint of
John Wiley & Sons, Inc., 605 Third Avenue, New York, NY 10158-0012*

British Library Cataloguing in Publication Data
A CIP catalogue record for this book is available from the
British Library

ISBN 1 85293 104 3 (UK)

Library of Congress Cataloging in Publication Data
A CIP catalog record for this book is available from the
Library of Congress

ISBN 0 470 219 48 3 (in the Americas only)

DB
983.7
.E69
1992

Typeset by Mayhew Typesetting, Rhayader, Powys
Printed and bound in Great Britain by Biddles Ltd., Guildford and King's Lynn

Contents

Contents

List of figures

List of tables

Preface

Few books have been published in English on Budapest, an old and important European city. Eminent books like *Budapest 1900*, the cultural history by John Lukács, are a rarity. There is particularly little information on urban life in the past forty years: government publications have listed data on the number of flats built or of hospital beds, but the life of the citizens of Budapest and its society have been overlooked.

The present volume considers the city as a macro-system that consists of three systems: the natural environment, the built environment and the society. The authors have focused primarily on the spatial aspects of the functioning of the society. A relatively detailed analysis of the mechanisms of urbanization in the state socialist system is given, which, we hope, will help to acquaint the western reader with the long-term processes of European urbanization under conditions of central planning, the specifities that have evolved, and how Central European traditions have been reflected.

We are particularly grateful to Professor Paul Knox, editor of the World Cities series, for including Budapest and for inviting us to write the book. We also wish to thank Vera Gáthy for translating the manuscript and Charles Hebbert for revising the English text. Thanks are also extended to Ágnes Spollár for typing the manuscript and compiling the bibliography, and to Piroska Dobi for drawing the maps.

György Enyedi and Viktória Szirmai
Budapest, January 1991

Part One

The urban environment

1
Introduction

The phrase 'Central European' in the subtitle of this book is not merely
a geographical definition. It refers to the fact that the Hungarian capital
is more than just the capital of a small country with 10.5 million
inhabitants: it is also the product of a larger area, of a particular European region: Central Europe. The Central European features, reflected
even in contemporary urban patterns, institutions and customs, are
mainly the products of the past 100 years. However, Budapest acquired
true significance during the course of its long history whenever it functioned as a centre of a region far larger than Hungary: Budapest was
elevated from among the urban centres of the eastern part of Europe by
the energies of Central Europe, and became the most important city east
of Vienna. When it was cut off from the resources of Central Europe by
historical events, the city shrank into insignificance and provincialism.
There are few big cities in Europe, the destiny of which have been so
strongly linked in this way to a larger region.

Budapest is in fact a young city under its present name. By 1872 the
three autonomous towns of Óbuda (literally, Old Buda), Buda and Pest
had already grown into one, and in that year were united administra-
tively as well. The capital stands on the site of one of the oldest
settlements in Europe. The archaeological finds at Castle Hill include the
tools and worked pieces of a pebble industry dating from 460,000 to
420,000 BC.

The first town, built by the Celts, occupied about 30 hectares along
the slopes of Gellért Hill (first century BC). It was called Ak Ink (mean-
ing 'spring rich in water'). Archaeological finds suggest that it may have
been a densely populated settlement, with a separate district of craftsmen
(potteries and bronze foundries). It may have been a trading centre as

3

well, as coins coming from different regions would indicate. The town was occupied by the Romans at the beginning of the Christian era. Its inhabitants moved to the Danube plains, to a city retaining the Celtic name (Aquincum), in the first century. In AD 106 the city became the capital of the province Pannonia Inferior. The headquarters of the governor and a significant military force were stationed here, and its population numbered about 20,000. It was frequently involved in wars on the border of the Roman Empire (formed by the Danube).

In the early fifth century the Roman defence lines were swept away by the Goths and other peoples fleeing westwards from the Huns. During the flourishing period of the Hun empire (after AD 430), this crossing point over the Danube retained its significance. No Romanized population remained in the city: they were replaced by Ostrogoths and Huns. In the 400 years following the dissolution of the Hun empire, the inhabitants of the territory of Hungary often changed in the turbulence of the Great Migration Era: Gepids, Longobards, Avars and other long-forgotten peoples of Germanic and Central Asian stock followed one another. Avar rule was the longest, lasting more than 200 years. The Avars were followed by the Franks, when the Danube again became the eastern borderline of a West European empire. In the ninth century Pannonia became part of the Moravian empire. There is no trace of any significant urban development during the Great Migration Era.

The Hungarians appeared around the end of the ninth century, establishing the seat of their prince near the crossing of the Danube. They quickly recognized the geostrategic significance of the place. Óbuda, the territory of the civilian city of Aquincum, became the first centre of Hungary. (The name Buda derives from a Hungarian given name; Pest is of Slavic origin, although it was a Muslim trading settlement in the tenth century.)

The princely (and later, royal) seat was moved to Esztergom in 973, and returned to Óbuda only in the thirteenth century. The Western European type of urban and bourgeois development began in Pest, which had a mixed German-Hungarian population in the thirteenth century.

In the middle of the thirteenth century, after the Tatar invasion, significant fortification work began all over the country. This was when the royal castle and the walled city were built on Castle Hill, on an elevated terrace of the Danube which could easily be defended. This third city was called Buda, its inhabitants presumably coming mainly from Pest. In the Middle Ages Buda gradually emerged from among the Hungarian towns, and it reached its peak in the second part of the fifteenth and the early sixteenth centuries. At that time the Hungarian kingdom extended over a large territory, including a significant part of the Balkans, and subsequently uniting with Poland and Lithuania. The rule of the Hungarian Crown extended from the Baltic to the Adriatic

Sea. The Hungarian kings established a highly centralized authority. While the German region of Europe was breaking up into small principalities in the late Middle Ages, a strong Hungarian empire was unfolding on the eastern side of Central Europe. Buda, the centre of the empire, was also a major urban settlement in political, as well as economic and cultural terms. At the turn of the fifteenth and sixteenth centuries Buda had 12–15,000 inhabitants, Pest 10,000, and Óbuda only 2–3,000. Thus the total population of the three towns that constitute the present Hungarian capital stood at roughly 25–30,000 – a big city in Central Europe in those days, ranking with Vienna, Prague, Cracow and Danzig. There was no urban centre of comparable significance in the Balkans. Moreover, no other city between Constantinople and Vienna had a population of over 5,000. The economic role of this centre was enhanced by the important trade routes crossing the Danube at Buda, linking Eastern and Western Europe together. Cattle for slaughter played an important role in East–West economic relations, driven from the grazing lands of the Hungarian Plain to the cities of northern Italy, Austria and Bavaria. Its role in the wine trade was also renowned. Miklós Oláh, Secretary to Queen Mária, wrote in 1536: 'The city of Buda is famous for the Italian, German, Polish, and recently even for the Turkish merchants, who gather here as if this place were the emporium of the whole of Hungary' (Horváth, *Budapest története* [The history of Budapest], vol. 2, p. 97). Attached to the royal seat, crafts were able to flourish in the city. The treasury made its purchases and the needs of the army were also partly met in Buda. This was where aristocrats and high priests had their houses and went shopping. Thus the great majority of craftsmen lived in Buda. A large number of German settlers were active in commerce and trade, and there were Armenian, Greek and even Arab merchants in the city. About half of the urban inhabitants may have been Hungarians. The cultural role of Buda was particularly significant during the reign of King Matthias. The Italian Renaissance had a great influence upon the city. The second Hungarian university was established in the city in 1395 (the first was founded in Pécs in 1367): and the first book was printed in Buda in 1473 under the title *Budai krónika* (The chronicle of Buda).

One-and-a-half centuries of prosperity was followed by a long decline. Buda and Pest came under Turkish occupation for about 150 years (and served as the headquarters of the Turkish military administration). That part of the country not occupied by the Turks became part of the Habsburg empire. When, at the end of the seventeenth century, Buda was liberated from Turkish rule, it became a provincial centre. When Buda was occupied, the Hungarian Diet moved to Pozsony (which since 1918 has belonged to Czechoslovakia, its Slovak name being Bratislava) and stayed there until 1848.

The urban environment

During the peaceful eighteenth century the total population began to grow, but the three cities only reached the size of their medieval population by the end of the century. However, a population of 35–40,000 was not considered a big city in the Europe of the late eighteenth century, nor did the city have any significant international role.

The nineteenth century was dominated by the Hungarians' struggle for independence and modernization. The national insurrection against the Habsburgs began in the Hungarian capital in 1848 and was defeated a little more than a year later. In 1867 the Habsburg administration reached a compromise with the Hungarian nobility, and Hungary was granted a status equal to that of Austria within the Habsburg empire. This made Budapest the twin capital of a dual monarchy. It was this compromise which opened the second great phase of development in the history of Budapest, lasting until World War I. This was the period of belated but rapid industrialization, urban growth and of catching up with the rest of Europe. The city never had such a glorious era before or since. Once again the city became the centre of a large region. As the capital of the Hungarian kingdom, which had a territory three times as large as today, it was the second most important urban centre of the Austro-Hungarian monarchy (after Vienna). And it had an economic and cultural influence stretching beyond the borders of the empire, to the Balkans and northern Italy. The population of the city trebled between 1875 and 1900. Of the large European cities, only Berlin recorded a similar rate of growth. When Óbuda, Buda and Pest were united, the Hungarian capital was a medium-sized city of 300,000 inhabitants, the seventeenth largest European city. In 1910, taking the present borders of the city, it already had a million inhabitants and ranked eighth in Europe, larger than Rome, Madrid or Milan. The rapid population growth fed upon all parts and nationalities of the monarchy. Migrants were attracted primarily by the vigorous industrial and economic boom. This was the age of the Hungarian industrial revolution, the benefits of which were mainly concentrated in Budapest. The city attracted the majority of newly-founded banks, business associations and industrial enterprises. The city's growth was closely linked to the expansion of industry. It was quite unusual for a big capital to have such a markedly industrial character. In 1910, 44 per cent of those employed worked in industry.

The unique geographical position of the capital played an important role in the development of the economy. The Hungarian railway network was built before the industrial revolution (in the 1850s). All the main railway lines radiated out from the capital in all directions across the Carpathian Basin, towards Vienna, the Adriatic, the Balkans and northern Europe. The development of the railway network around Budapest was influenced primarily by political considerations: the Hungarian capital – politically still subordinate to Vienna – wanted to secure its control over the Carpathian Basin. Moreover, since the construction of railways was heavily subsidized, the railway lines were soon acquired by the state, so that national strategic considerations could determine where the lines were laid. The various railway lines met at the navigable section of the Danube, at the largest river port: Budapest. It became an entrepôt for raw materials, like timber and grain, and was where the products of an enormous agricultural hinterland were processed, stored and sold. According to some estimates, it was the world's second largest centre of the milling industry early this century. Profits from the export of agricultural products of the Hungarian Plain all found their way to the commercial centre. Up-to-date engineering and electrical works also appeared, and by the beginning of the twentieth century Budapest had become a centre of modern large-scale industry.

This rapid growth was very different from the urban growth of developing countries today. The inflowing labour quickly found employment and adjusted to urban society within a single generation. As the population grew, so the city expanded, and new residential suburbs were built. During the last decades of the nineteenth century the city grew at a rate which has never been matched since, even during the reconstruction after World War II.

So fast was this growth that it earned the description of an 'American tempo'. However, Budapest resembled Chicago only in the speed of its growth. The development was carefully planned and the effect was delightful. In 1870 the municipality set up the Council of Public Works, which elaborated a grand master plan, and the city had the power to realize it. Everything that marked the standards of the age could be found in the master plan: there was a system of ring roads and boulevards, and a network of urban public transport: the height of the buildings was set, green spaces were included, and so forth. Though a major part of the city was built within the space of twenty years, the result was not monotony but a harmonious uniform style.

During recent years it has become fashionable to discover the legacy of the turn of the century. Vienna has become particularly fashionable for art nouveau, psychoanalysis, Viennese music, and its delightful decline as the capital of the dual monarchy. It is not generally known, however, that Budapest also had an intellectual boom at the turn of the century. The young Bartók and Gustav Mahler were teaching at the Academy of Music at the same time, and the magnificent buildings of the Hungarian art nouveau were completed in quick succession. In Vienna, decay could be felt in its intellectual life: the imperial city was rooted in the political power of the monarchy, but this power had been already weakened. In Budapest, however, there was no sense of decay. The city was feeding upon the growth of the Hungarian economy which still had great *élan*. Rapid development suppressed the sense of danger. Budapest was a dynamic, extremely optimistic city right until the final collapse. The modern infrastructural development of the city was most impressive. Bridges were built over the Danube, and the first underground railway of the European continent was opened here in 1896. In 1873 electric lighting was brought to the streets. In 1887 trams appeared, followed in 1888 by the first suburban trains; in 1885 the first urban telephone exchange was installed; in 1896 the Post Office used battery-driven vans for delivering parcels; and in 1900 the Royal Hungarian Automobile Club was founded. Within a few decades the capital was, it seemed, making up for the long centuries it had spent behind the rest of Europe. However, this rapid progress was founded on fragile foundations. The capital could not rely on a broadly modernizing Hungarian urban network, and had to join the main trend of European urban development on its own. In 1910 it was a big city of 1 million inhabitants, while the population of the second and third largest country towns (Szeged and Szabadka) was only just over 100,000, both of them traditional agricultural market towns.

The First World War and its consequences are well known. The Austro-Hungarian monarchy was broken up. Budapest became the oversized capital of a small country, which could not regain its earlier international role in a hostile Carpathian Basin that had been cut into pieces. Its population continued to grow at a moderate pace, but it now resembled the urban growth of the developing countries, nurtured more by crisis in the countryside than by the internal energy of the city. By the 1930s Budapest was beginning to overcome the consequences of World War I, when the next world war overwhelmed it, causing enormous damage to its buildings, as well as to its population. Under socialism, it has maintained a steady rate of development. With the dissolution of socialism in 1989, the city has entered the post-industrial age with the leading role of blue-collar industry being replaced by services and a white-collar workforce. The changes that have taken place in the urban society of the past forty years are presented in greater detail in subsequent chapters of this book. In 1991, as these lines are being written, Budapest is again searching for its place among the major European metropolises. Budapest is once again becoming a Central European capital.

2
The physical environment and environmental problems

Physical geography

Geographical location

The view from the top of Gellért Hill gives a striking first impression of the city. The curving Danube, the green islands and bridges, the massed houses in Pest, the houses spreading out across the wooded hills of Buda, and the Castle Hill with its royal palace are all evidence of the fortunate position of the city. However, the location of a city is hardly a matter of luck. Large cities only evolve and survive for centuries in locations where the geographical conditions are particularly favourable for human settlement. These conditions either stem from local, natural resources (local energy), or from the potential of the geographical location.

The local resources of Budapest are favourable, but not particularly rich. In medieval times, and at the time of the extensive construction at the end of the nineteenth century, the abundance of wood, stone and clay suitable for bricklaying proved a great advantage. However, the city does not have the raw materials that industry requires. (The small Eocene coal deposits have already been exhausted in the vicinity of the city.) Its water resources are very important: supplies of drinking water are abundant, and there is the river and also some medicinal spas. So the local resources favoured the initial settlement, but did not justify the evolution of a metropolitan area.

The main factor in Budapest's growth was its location within the Carpathian Basin. The Carpathian Basin is divided by the Danube. Any

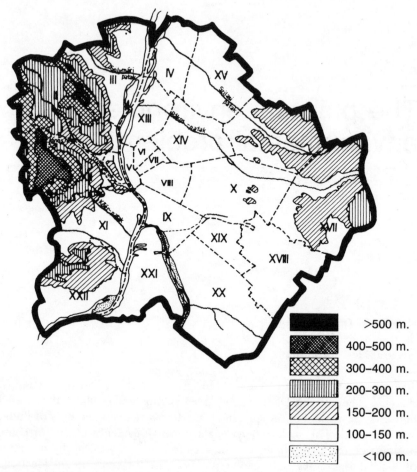

Figure 2.1 Relief and rivers (altitude above sea level)

political power intending to control the region had to locate its centre on the Danube, at a crossing point that could easily be defended. The centre of the Hungarian kingdom that controlled the Carpathian Basin for a thousand years could not have developed anywhere else.

The Danube emerges from the Hungarian Central Mountains north of Budapest in a broad, slightly sloping alluvial cone. The city was built between two big islands, those of Szentendre and Csepel. The river bed narrows at Budapest and offers an easy crossing. Leaving the mountains, the water slows down, so that the many shallows on the river bed made it a suitable crossing point for animals and for people in leather bags in the early Middle Ages. (These leather bags acted like life-jackets; they were filled with air and used for crossing shallow rivers with short deep parts.) With the river cutting deep into the alluvial cone, its banks were safe from floods, barring exceptional years. The next good crossing point was far to the south on account of the high right bank and the marshy Danube valley, which placed it out on the periphery of the Carpathian Basin.

Another factor in the city's location was its position at the meeting point of three large landscape units: the Hungarian Central Mountains, that form the inner mountain zone of the Carpathians, the hills of Transdanubia, and the Great Hungarian Plain. By the Middle Ages the Danube was a trading route with the Balkans.

The city is located at 47° 29' north and 19° 9' east. It is in the centre of the European continent: 3,000 km. from the easternmost point of Europe (in the Ural Mountains), and 2,500 km. from the westernmost (in Portugal). It is only half as far from the southernmost (1,300 km.), as from the northernmost point (2,600 km.)

The surface

The Danube separates two different regions from each other. The right bank of the Danube is hilly, as the western part of the city is occupied by the cut up block-mountains called the Buda Hills, the highest point of which is the János Hill at 529 m. above sea level. The left bank is flat, an alluvial cone of about 100 m. above sea level, a legacy of the Pleistocene Danube.

During the early settlements the right bank offered more advantages. The hills were covered by forests abundantly stocked with game. The mountain range was broken by small basins and valleys which the long-distance trade routes followed to reach the ferry over the Danube at Gellért Hill. These routes still constitute the main elements of Buda's road network. In the thirteenth century the Castle Hill (a steep river terrace above the Danube) was best suited for the construction of the walled city and the royal palace. The hilly regions of the Buda side could be defended more easily, so that Buda was the most important of the three cities in the Middle Ages.

The Buda Hills are mainly built of Triassic limestone and dolomite. This thick layer of limestone – and dolomite – penetrating to a depth of 800 metres was deposited some 200 million years ago by the sea, which covered the present location of the city. On this territory sandstone (Hárshegy), Oligocene clay and marl, soft-water limestone and Pleistocene loess can be found. The dominance of limestone and dolomite is the cause of several karstic phenomena: there are about fifty karstic caves in the mountain range, and the region is poor in surface water. Of these caves, the most spacious passages are to be found in the Pálvölgyi stalactite caves: more than 1 kilometre in length, they have been developed as a tourist attraction.

The urban environment

On the Pest side, the flat left bank started to develop rapidly from the eighteenth century, particularly from the beginning of the industrial revolution. The flat lie of the land suited establishments requiring space, such as industrial estates, warehouses, stores and housing estates. The ports of the Danube were also developed on the Pest side, together with the related institutions of commercial and processing activities.

Before the eighteenth century, Pest – the heart of the present city – was built high enough to be safe from floods and was surrounded by a marshy branch of the Danube. Two flood levels and five terraces free of floods developed on the plain of Pest out of river sand and gravel. Pest was also surrounded by a city wall (along the line of the present 'little' boulevard), and highways to the surrounding towns (Vác, Kecskemét, Hatvan) run out from its gates. The basis of the Pest street plan is constituted by these highways, the city wall and the boulevards that followed the line of the old dried-up branch of the Danube.

The seasons in Budapest

We cannot resist the temptation to quote some passages from John Lukács's book *Budapest 1900*, describing the seasons.

In Budapest, the contrast of the seasons, and of their colours, is sharper than in Vienna. Violet in Budapest is a spring colour, it is the custom to present tiny bouquets of the first violets to women as early as March. In March, too, comes the sound and the smell of the rising river. The Danube runs swifter and higher in Budapest than in Vienna. It would often flood the lower quays, and the sound and sight of that swirling mass of water would be awesome. By the end of April a pearly haze would bathe the bend of the river and the bridges and quays, rising to Castle Hill . . .

May and June in Budapest have something near Mediterranean about them. The chairs and tables were put out in front of the cafes and in the open-air restaurants. The freshness of the dustless air, especially after the May showers, brought the presence of the Hungarian countryside into the city . . .

Summer is hot, sultry at times, broken by tremendous thunderstorms but almost never damp. When the dark thunderheads convened high over the dry, dusty streets, they carried the promise of relief and the return of the long pleasant summer evenings, for the evenings were almost always cool . . .

Autumn can be a short season in Budapest: in any event, its beauties are unpredictable, like those of rapidly maturing women . . . March is the cruelest month in Budapest: and November is the saddest. The fog swirled around the broad pillars of the Danube bridges, it rose to cloud the high hills of Buda. On All Souls' Day thousands of people streamed toward the cemeteries of Budapest, with flowers in their hands, on that holiday which is perhaps taken more seriously in Hungary than elsewhere because of the national temperament . . . The greatest tragedies in the history of modern Hungary – the hanging of thirteen martyr Hungarian generals after the collapse of the War of Independence in 1849, the collapse of the ancient monarchy in the defeat of the First World War in 1918, the collapse of the effort to free Hungary from its deadly alliance with Hitler's Reich in 1944, the collapse of the great national rising in 1956 – all happened in October or early November . . .

And then, one morning – it would come as early as the third week of November, and surely before the middle of December –, the sky was gray but rich, great flakes of snow were coming down all over Budapest: a celestial filling, like the goose down in the comforters of its bedrooms. (Lukács, 1988, pp. 10–13.)

A geographic description of the capital's climate is far drier. The mean annual temperature is +11°C over the past fifty years. The coldest month is January (–0.8°C), and the hottest is July (21.9°C). The difference in mean temperature between the coldest and hottest months is just above 22°C, on the verge of a continental climate. As we have seen, the four seasons are markedly different, and the climate of the capital is formed by the effect of four different climatic systems. The continental and Arctic air-masses are mainly effective in winter; their frequency is about 65 per cent in January. In summer and autumn the Atlantic effect is strongest, while in spring and in autumn a subtropical (Mediterranean) effect can be noted. The effect of these four climatic types assert themselves differently each year, so that each year shows considerable variation.

It is interesting that the climate is highly varied even within the relatively small territory of the city, according to the surface and the density of construction. For instance, there is more than 100 mm. difference in the annual rainfall (with an average of 611 mm.) between the Buda Hills and the plain of Pest, and the mean temperature for July shows a difference of almost 3°C within the city. In winter the inner parts of the city are about 2.5°C warmer than the higher parts of the Buda Hills.

The dominant winds are from the north-west bringing clean air from the Buda Hills. The largest industrial zone of the capital has developed in the south-eastern part of the city, which is a favourable location in terms of air pollution. The frequency of the south-eastern winds, blowing industrial pollution towards the city centre, is 10 per cent (of windy days).

The waters of the city

Water has a tremendous significance in the life of the city. Here, of course, the River Danube takes prominence. The historical role of the river has already been mentioned. The Danube is an indispensable part of the life of the modern metropolitan city as well: it supplies industrial water, and – indirectly – drinking water. It receives the sewage of the city, and in parts its banks serve the purposes of recreation and rest. The city is located 1,200 km. from its source, and 1,600 km. from the estuary. Before river control, occasional floods destroyed the city. The floods of 1838 caused particular damage. At that time a number of partly dried up beds of the river still lay within the city.

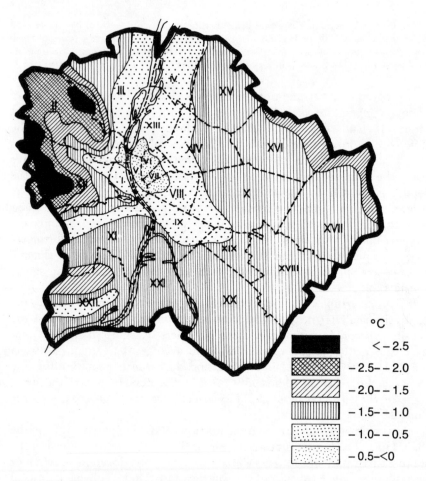

Figure 2.2 Mean temperature of the coldest month (January)

The regulation of the Danube within the city was started in the 1870s. During this work the river bed was considerably narrowed (thus creating land for construction), the shallows were removed, and the embankments and quays were developed. The quays were completed in 1909. This forced the Danube between high retaining banks, which almost totally eliminated any danger of floods. At present the length of the flood-prevention lines in the capital is 82 km. The ports of the Danube were developed on the Pest side, and the warehouses stretched almost to the present city centre. In 1927, a modern port with a custom-free zone was built on Csepel Island.

The drinking and industrial water requirements of the city are met, directly or indirectly, by the river. Drinking water is obtained from wells sunk into the gravel bed of the Danube, where ground water is in contact

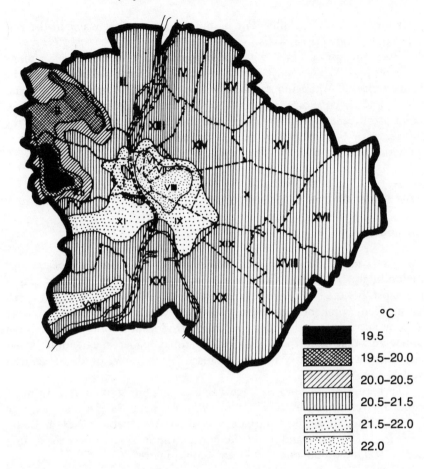

	°C
■	19.5
▨	19.5–20.0
▨	20.0–20.5
▥	20.5–21.5
⣿	21.5–22.0
⠂	22.0

Figure 2.3 Mean temperature in the warmest month (July)

with the river, and where the gravel layer works as a natural filter. A number of rivulets reach the Danube through the territory of the capital. The streams from the Buda side are short and seasonal. The most significant is the Ördögárok, which has been covered. The tributaries of the Pest side are longer, with a wider catchment area and a more regular quantity of water (the Rákos creek is the most significant), supplying water for irrigation in the vegetable plots up until a few decades ago.

A number of medicinal spas lie along the tectonic break along the bed of the Danube. More than 100 natural spas and thirteen artesian wells at seventeen locations yield lukewarm or warm medicinal water within the capital. Hot water gushes forth from great depths (1,500–2,000 m.) through the crevices in the rocks. Their temperature and yield is practically constant. Hot water rushes up in three areas in the periphery of the Buda Hills. The baths and artesian hot water of the Pest side come from bored wells.

These hot springs laid the foundations of a culture of baths many centuries ago. While today only the ruins of the large public baths of the Roman city of Aquincum can be seen, some Turkish baths from the sixteenth and seventeenth centuries are still operating. The medicinal spas are a significant tourist attraction and may become even more so in the future, as it is rare to find such a variety of medicinal spas combined with the attraction of a large city.

The state of the environment

Air pollution

The city cannot always be seen from the top of Gellért Hill because of the pollutants in the air. Comparative data show that Budapest is one of the most polluted of European cities today. Air pollution is the city's greatest environmental problem. The two worst offenders are sulphur dioxide and nitrogen dioxide. The concentration of sulphur dioxide is ten times, and that of nitrogen dioxide five times higher in Budapest's inner city than in the countryside. It is caused by industry, outdated vehicles and heating systems.

The permitted 24-hour average value of sulphur dioxide is 0.15 mg./cubic metre of air. According to 1980–81 data the 24-hour average concentration of sulphur dioxide was 0.061 mg./cubic metre in Budapest. In 1987, 1988 and 1989 the concentration slightly decreased, falling to 0.058, 0.050 and 0.053 mg./cubic metre.

Figure 2.4 shows that the average concentration of sulphur dioxide has decreased during the past sixteen years, mainly because heating systems have been modernized. However, differentiation across the city is rather significant, according to the surveys of the Municipal Service of Public Health and Epidemics. In 1989 pollution was much higher in the industrial zone, reaching 0.125 mg./cubic metre.

The permitted average value of nitrogen dioxide over a 24-hour period is 0.085 mg./cubic metre. According to 1980–81 surveys, the 24-hour average value of nitrogen dioxide concentration was 0.040 mg./cubic metre. It reached 0.080 in 1987, and 0.086 in 1988, and stood at 0.119 mg./cubic metre in 1989. The highest nitrogen dioxide concentrations are in the inner parts of the city and in some outer industrial districts parallel to and east of the Pest bank of the Danube. Here, values as high as 0.300 mg./cubic metre may occur.

During the past few years carbon monoxide levels have significantly grown along the boulevards and avenues (KÖJÁL, 1990). The highest

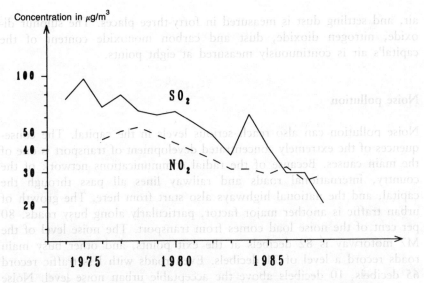

Figure 2.4 Average annual concentration of SO$_2$ and NO$_2$ measured in the atmosphere of Budapest

annual average was measured at Baross Square, where in 1987 it was 5.2, in 1988 5.7, and in 1989 it was 7.8 mg./cubic metre. The hydrocarbon (non-methane) pollution of the main traffic of the capital is also significant, five times the North American norm.

The annual average of settling dust is 150 tons/sq. kilometre. The quantity of settling dust may reach the annual average of 200–240 tons/sq. kilometre at times in the most dust-polluted parts of the city. Surface lead is still around the internationally accepted norms. But lead pollution far surpasses the Hungarian norm around the major crossroads because of road transport. The highest lead pollution can be found at the crossroads of Mártírok Street and Keleti Károly Street, and in the tunnel linking the areas of inner Buda and Krisztinaváros.

It should be noted that there are many uncertainties in the measurement of air pollution. Emission data are based on self-declarations made by polluters. Instruments are out of date and the international comparison of the results cannot be guaranteed. Air pollution (emission) is measured by the Institute of Environmental Protection located in Budapest, and by its stations in the country. The spread of materials polluting the air is measured by the National Meteorological Service. Air quality (immission) has been analysed by the Station of Public Health and Epidemics under the guidance of the National Institute of Public Health since 1974. Fifty-two measuring stations operate in Budapest with phased sampling. Twenty-four measuring stations in the network, the so-called Regional Emission Testing Network, analyse the condition of the air, and settling dust is measured in forty-three places. The sulphur dioxide, nitrogen dioxide, dust and carbon monoxide content of the capital's air is continuously measured at eight points.

Noise pollution

Noise pollution can also reach serious levels in the capital. The consequences of the extremely concentrated development of transport is one of the main causes. Because of the radial communications network of the country, international roads and railway lines all pass through the capital, and the national highways also start from here. The growth of urban traffic is another major factor, particularly along busy roads. 80 per cent of the noise load comes from transport. The noise level of the M7 motorway is 82 decibels at the exit points, and other busy main roads record a level of 71 decibels. Even roads with less traffic record 65 decibels, 10 decibels above the acceptable urban noise level. Noise from the recently-extended Ferihegy airport near the city is a serious problem for the neighbouring parts of the city and for some suburban areas.

The problem of waste

20 million cubic metres of solid waste develop annually in the settlements of Hungary, 25 per cent of it in Budapest. About 4 million cubic metres is communal solid waste, the rest coming from industry. The majority of the dumping grounds developed in former clay and sand pits are almost exhausted. Ground water conditions make the establishment of new dumps difficult. Already, about 10 per cent of the accumulating solid waste is being dumped illegally.

The quantity of potential secondary raw materials has increased within the waste accumulating in the capital, as have hazardous materials. These are mainly chemicals, pesticides, paint, chemical materials used for handicrafts, etc. The recycling of household garbage has not taken off, although this has been tried in the capital. Selection is made impossible by the existing system of collection, by the storage of garbage in houses, and by the lack of any technical solutions. Garbage has been taken away from all homes with a closed-system, dust-free technology since 1976. Theoretically, industry should be able to implement selective technologies successfully applied elsewhere. However, it is not yet prepared to recycle. An incinerator utilizing waste has been operating in the capital since 1981 which eliminates 30 per cent of the solid waste. The installation of a second incinerator with an annual capacity of 300,000 tons is being prepared.

In Budapest 210,000 tons of hazardous waste is produced annually by the factories, according to their own records. Until 1982, the problem of the collection, treatment and neutralization of hazardous wastes was ignored. A large proportion of the dangerous wastes were deposited at illegal sites and dumping grounds, were let into the surface waters, or were burnt. In that year the government decided upon the development of a national storage network of dangerous wastes: the construction of two incinerators, three deposits for dangerous waste, and nineteen transitory storage facilities in the counties. Because of financial problems and the conflicting interests of the counties, but mainly as a result of the protests by local populations, only one incinerator could be built, in the town of Dorog, 40 km. from Budapest. A permanent storage site was completed in the vicinity of Aszód, about the same distance from the capital but outside the catchment area of the Danube. The introduction of methods for the utilization of dangerous waste would be very important, as would the construction of a national network for handling such wastes.

The problem of water supply

The quality of the Danube's water is vital to the life of the entire city. The river and its gravel terraces represent the drinking water base, particularly the wells drained along the banks. About 90 per cent of drinking water is produced by the wells located on the Szentendre Island to the north, and the Csepel Island to the south. The waterworks of the capital produce the remaining 10 per cent. Wells further away from the Danube had to be closed down because of the danger posed by the growing nitrate content.

When the river reaches the city, it is already polluted. The quality of water falls into the 'polluted' category (Class II – according to the Hungarian classification, which means that treatment is necessary before the water is suitable for use: the ecosystem suffers from, but is not destroyed by, the pollution) at the northern point of the capital; in the southern part it comes into the 'heavily polluted' classification (Class III – water quality cannot be restored even by treatment methods: pollution is considered detrimental to the ecosystem itself). It is clear from the comparison of the data north and south of Budapest that the quality of the Danube water is adversely affected by the capital. The polluting effect of the big city can be seen primarily in mercury and lead levels. In addition, the bacteriological components are worse below the city (1,659 river km.) than above it (1,631 river km.) (1985 data). A definite deterioration has been recorded in the bacteriological content during the past decade. Between 1970 and 1974 the frequency of 'heavily polluted' condition was 20 to 40 per cent north of Budapest, and 69 to 70 per cent south of it. Between 1985 and 1988 the frequency grew to 86–93 per cent south of the capital (Bulla, 1989, p. 76). The small streams of the capital and the smaller rivulets coming from the territory of Pest county reach the city even more polluted than the Danube.

The sewage of the capital is sent into the Danube. The daily average quantity of communal and industrial waste-water is almost 1 million cubic metres. Only 7 per cent is mechanically treated and 13 per cent reaches the river without any filtration. Sewage and the treatment of waste-water are the least developed of the capital's public utilities. Industrial waste-water also represents a grave problem. Of the 1,500 industrial plants emitting dangerous waste-water, only 424 have pre-treatment equipment, half of which were installed before 1970, and so are out of date.

Environmental damage, by zones

The different zones of the city struggle with different ecological problems. The city centre of Pest faces problems of dense building, a lack of green space, transport difficulties and air pollution. The Buda regions used to be the calmer, quieter parts of the city, and the air was cleaner even after World War II. Today the inner parts of Buda suffer from the same ecological damage as the inner area of Pest, and especially from the problems of transport and air pollution.

Figure 2.5 represents the average 24-hour sulphur dioxide and nitrogen dioxide concentration of the zones of the capital. It can be clearly seen that the inner zone and the neighbouring parts of the city, the belt between the Grand Boulevard and the Small Boulevard, and the industrial parts of the transitory (mixed industrial/residential) zone are very polluted. Besides air pollution from the industries wedged into residential areas, the traffic in narrow streets and high noise levels, further problems are posed by the poor-quality housing stock and the lack of green space. There are 1,760 industrial plants located within residential areas.

The industrial suburbs and peripheral districts, such as Újpest, Nagytétény and Csepel are characterized by damage similar to that in the transitory zone because of the large number of polluting industrial plants. Heavy metal pollution is above average in the vicinity of the Metal-lokémia Plant of Nagytétény and the Csepel Works. The abandoned clay pits and quarries present a greater problem, though recultivation has begun in many cases. The adverse effects deriving from the lack of public utilities, together with soil pollution, are concentrated in peripheral districts. Soil pollution is known with precision only at certain points within the city. Dumping grounds, including illegal ones, are also located in this sub-region.

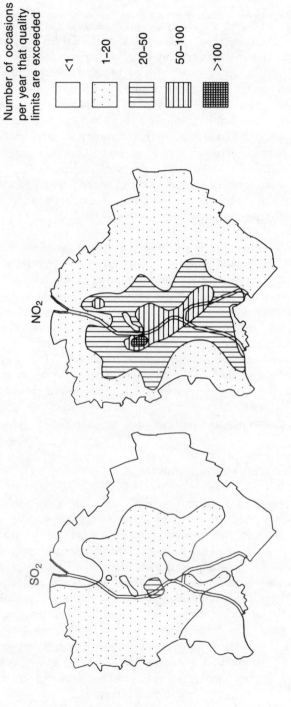

Number of occasions per year that quality limits are exceeded

☐	<1
▫	1–20
▤	20–50
▥	50–100
▦	>100

NO₂

SO₂

Figure 2.5 Atmospheric concentration of sulphur dioxide and nitrogen dioxide in Budapest

The urban environment

Health problems

In Hungary, the number of deaths has exceeded the number of births since 1980. During the past two decades, death caused by cardiovascular and malignant diseases has sharply increased, particularly for young and middle-aged men. The annual cost of health problems attributable to environmental causes is estimated at about 35.5 thousand million Forints on the basis of data from 1986 and 1988. This is about 4 per cent of the 1986 Gross National Product (Bulla, 1989, p. 202).

In the densely-populated inner parts of Budapest, the mortality rate of the male population is much higher and its life expectancy is five years shorter than that in some rural zones. The difference between life expectancy in the 'best' green belt and the 'worst' inner district is as great as the difference in the mortality rates of the male population of an industrially advanced country, like Germany, and of a less advanced one, like Syria.

Ecological problems have a differential impact upon the various social and occupational groups, though hardly anyone is free from all adverse effects. About 11 per cent of the population of the capital lives under very favourable, and about 34 per cent under favourable environmental conditions. These are mostly groups located in better regions who have higher incomes, are better educated, and are less exposed to health hazards of ecological origin. About one-quarter of the inhabitants live in particularly problematic environmental conditions. The socially handicapped, uneducated and unskilled social layers are highly represented, being more exposed to environmental harm because of their unfavourable lifestyle with homes in a worse ecological position. In their case the social and environmental disadvantages are cumulative.

Causes of environmental problems

Some environmental hazards are the inevitable corollaries of modern urban development. In the late 1950s and early 1960s, West European and American cities had to face ecological challenges similar to those facing Hungary today. However, in those societies financial resources were available for handling ecological problems, and there were democratic institutions and movements which could ensure the solution or mitigation of ecological conflicts. In Hungary, these economic resources are not available, since the socialist economy was unable to produce them. The economic development of the 1950s and 1960s, with its emphasis on energy-consuming heavy industry, had a strong impact on the natural environment. Environmental damage was particularly bad in the industrial regions: in the new towns that grew up around the coal mining, metallurgical and heavy chemical industries, and in Budapest.

Ecological problems that resulted from this concentrated, inefficient and polluting industrial production were made still worse by the state socialist management of society, and the functioning mechanisms of the redistributive political structure. Centralized management continuously ignored ecological interests both in their decision-making and in the distribution of central financial resources, because of political, ideological and power considerations. The social forces most interested in the protection of the natural environment and human health, such as local authorities, were given no voice.

A number of legal norms have since been introduced, and measures taken, in the interests of environmental protection, particularly since the 1970s. The most significant was the Protection of the Human Environment Act, passed by the National Assembly in 1976. In 1980 the Council of Ministers approved the National Concept and Set of Requirements for the Protection of the Environment, which safeguards the implementation of the Act. Following the development of the national regulations, the government ordered the elaboration of a long-term concept and a detailed set of requirements by ministers and heads of national authorities in their respective fields. It reflected the hierarchical management of society that only local, and especially county, concepts and that of the capital could be subsequently elaborated. The city council only worked out its long-term concept for environmental protection for the municipal area of Budapest. The council approved the concept, which covers the period up to the year 2000, in 1982 (The Long Term Concept of Environmental Protection of Budapest, 1982).

However, no significant changes have taken place despite new legislation, while environmental hazards have increased in the past decade. Local councils, which in theory were empowered to enforce the law, are partly dependent for their finances on the polluting industrial plants. This limited their ability to act; nor was there a social basis for any such action.

Under state socialism, ecological data were not published. Even the intelligentsia only rarely heard about the gravity of ecological problems. The experts had no easy access to the results of environmental monitoring, as the more important data were classified. Democratic institutions were lacking because of the nature of the political system, and ecological movements were not permitted. All of this resulted in a situation very different from that in advanced western societies, and produced special ecological problems in addition to the damage caused by urbanization.

The urban environment

Conditions for change

Ecological movements burst forth with increasing frequency in places like Ajka, Százhalombatta, Dorog, Ófalu and a number of other country settlements from the late 1970s onwards. In Budapest, the most significant intellectual ecological movement in this period was the Danube Circle, which was born to protest against the Bős-Nagymaros River Dam System. (In 1977, the Czechoslovak and Hungarian governments signed an agreement for the establishment of a complex hydropower scheme on the Danube north of Budapest.) The pace of construction on the Hungarian side was slow and the work was finally suspended by the last Communist government in 1989 in response to strong civil protests. In 1990, the new freely-elected Parliament decided on the final cancellation of the project for ecological reasons (dismantlement will require further negotiations with the Czechoslovakian government). Beyond ecological matters, the movement also represented other interests: the demand for political change and the intelligentsia's desire for autonomy.

Ecological sensitivity has grown among the population as they either learn about environmental hazards from the media, or experience them themselves personally. In certain crisis situations, ecological sensitivity may be the key determining factor in the behaviour of social groups.

In the early 1990s, the initial stage of the transition to democracy offered the chance to improve the ecological situation. The organization of civil society, the legitimation and strengthening of ecological movements, the free access to ecological information, and the rebirth of local government are significant preconditions for the representation of ecological interests. However, the improvement of the natural environment is a realistic possibility only if the material resources for environmental protection are created; if the economic difficulties of the country decrease; if a strong middle class evolves that is responsive to an environmentally-friendly way of life, and is able to afford it; and if a broad social consensus evolves over the judgement of ecological issues.

Today the situation is far more problematic: the ecological challenge faces a Hungarian society which is in the midst of a deep recession, when neither a strong middle class has evolved, nor a social consensus established. There is still no agreement on how strongly ecological considerations can assert themselves within the government: moreover, it is not even known how the ecological interests of various groups can be accommodated in the bargaining process, or which social segments would stand to gain. Even the distribution of financial resources for environmental protection between the state and local government has not yet been decided upon. And since social pressure is lacking, the political parties do not pay serious attention to the issue.

3
Urban landscapes

Any traveller familiar with the metropolises of the world can immediately feel at home in Budapest, where much of the architecture is a simple adaptation of styles that are found the world over. Yet there are many buildings that have a character specific to Budapest. A number of factors have shaped the city's architecture, first and foremost being its geographical location. The great beauty of Budapest derives from its relationship to the Danube, from the special coexistence that is not to be found in any other city located on a river. Both Paris and Prague span rivers, and the same River Danube flows through Vienna. Yet the river is not as primary an element in the view of that city as it is in Budapest. The panorama of the Danube links the hills of Buda to the mass of the city extending over the plains of Pest. That Budapest was the product of the merger of three cities also had important architectural consequences, embracing within one boundary a number of separate yet connected parts.

As we have seen above, this merger occurred during a period of dynamic urban development. However, this growth destroyed the achievements of earlier historical periods and wiped out their architectural works. Little remains of the rather provincial yet elegant Classicist city of the early nineteenth century. No other large European city belongs to such an extent and so uniformly to the age of architectural Eclecticism. In Budapest the late-nineteenth-century architectural environment acquired a special significance. Paris and Vienna developed into great metropolises during the same period. But since they already had a significant older core, the new additions did not dominate the character of the city. In Budapest, the lack of an older centre gave the new developments in the city far greater prominence.

1 Belváros (The Inner City)
2 Erzsébetváros
3 Terézváros
4 Lipótváros
5 Viziváros
6 Vár
7 Tabán
8 Krisztinaváros

Figure 3.1 The names of parts of Budapest

The third factor shaping the architectural environment was the location of Budapest between Eastern and Western Europe. Its architecture often displayed a rootlessness, copying various Eastern and Western architectural trends according to the prevailing influences upon the country.

To consider the architecture of the city, let us break the city up into smaller units with the help of the maps and photographs included in this volume. The best view for 'sightseeing' is offered by Gellért Hill. From here you can see the Danube River dissecting the city in two. On the left bank lies Pest, its older inner city surrounded by the Small Boulevard, and the present city spreading across the Grand Boulevard and other major avenues. From here you can see the tall apartment blocks of the first 'ring' around the edge of the inner city, and the outline of the second 'ring' of apartment buildings in the distance. And you can see the Danube flowing down from the north in several branches, embracing the Ship-yard Island and Margit (Margaret) Island, as it broadens and narrows. It reaches its narrowest point at Gellért Hill, after which the river once again divides into branches. But dominating the view from Gellért Hill is Castle Hill, and so we will take this as our starting point.

The Castle district

The Castle district is located on Castle Hill in Buda, on the right side of the Danube as it flows through the city. The late Pál Granasztói, the eminent architect, described this as a reversed Acropolis. The acropolises were usually built first, with those seeking shelter and security only settling at their foot later. Castle Hill in Buda was a barren hill until the Mongol invasion of the thirteenth century. It was the population of Pest, after the town had been destroyed by the Mongols, who migrated there to found a new town for themselves.

The royal household occupied the southern tip of the hill, where the Castle was built. The significance of the royal Castle was greatest during the reign of King Sigismund in the 1400s, and subsequently under King Matthias Corvinus, when it became the centre of the royal administration until 1541.

By the end of the Middle Ages Buda, with its royal palace and Gothic city, was one of the famous centres of Europe. However, Turkish rule between 1541 and 1686 destroyed the Castle area. Contemporary accounts say that only the debris of the palaces survived after the expulsion of the Turks. However, the medieval urban structure remained intact.

Italian architects participated in the reconstruction and surveying work of the post-1686 period. The impact of Italian architecture appears not only in the atmosphere of the small palaces, but also in the later trends of Hungarian architecture. The Church played a major role in the reconstruction, and a significant part of public construction served ecclesiastical and military purposes. The Jesuit order settled down here, and introduced the baroque style in attitudes toward daily life, in the social festivities, and in architecture. It was at that time that the modest baroque Royal Palace was built, although it no longer served as a royal residence. In the eighteenth century a larger palace was built. Baroque features can still be seen in some ecclesiastical buildings and in certain residential buildings.

Hungarian Classicism, which unfolded in the first decades of the nineteenth century during the early Reform period, made its impact on the residential buildings of the aristocracy. However, in the burghers' city attached to the palace the majority of the residential buildings were simple, solid, plastered houses. There were light sunlit cobbled streets, lined with low buildings with narrow but lively courtyards. The medieval sedilia at the entrances of these courtyards recall the way of life of those days – the leisure and customs of travellers, availing themselves of the inns offered by the city. The layout of the streets and squares was determined not by some geometrical principle, but by topography. There are hardly any houses that are identical; almost every house varies in the curve of its roof, the width of its gate or the smoothness of its wall. The Castle district is beautiful and simple. It was built by burghers and masons, in keeping with the demands of rationalism, alongside the buildings of the Church and the aristocracy.

The architecture of the twentieth century has significantly transformed the character of Castle Hill. Classicism raised two-storeyed, Romanticism three-storeyed, and Eclecticism four-storeyed buildings in the Castle area. But the turn of the century and the second part of the twentieth century saw the construction of larger apartment blocks on the sides of Castle Hill. A number of taller public buildings, including ministries and the National Archives, were also built there, disrupting both the medieval structure and the baroque outlines of the district.

The siege of the Castle during World War II inflicted great damage on the district and the palace. During the reconstruction, efforts were made to retain the architectural traditions of the Royal Palace and the baroque outlines, and to rebuild the dome. The palace took on a new role: it now houses museums, the National Library, the National Gallery, and the Central Archives. Restrictions were imposed on the height of the taller buildings. The decorative architecture of the Matthias Church and the Fishermen's Bastion are major attractions in the district. The new Hotel Hilton, utilizing the medieval façade of the Dominican monastery, was a new colourful addition to the district in the 1970s and gave a boost to tourism. Many believe that the Castle district has a style of its own, and that certain buildings do not fit in. But in fact the Castle district only had a consistent architectural style in the Middle Ages and the baroque period. Later this was lost as each period added its own architecture and style. Consequently the Castle district has no unified style, only a unified history.

The Tabán, the Viziváros and the Krisztinaváros

The Tabán, or Ráczváros (Serbian city), is situated between Castle Hill, the Naphegy, and Gellért Hill. In 1212 Andrew II, King of Hungary issued a decree which referred to this old part of Buda as the Tabán. Tabán means foothill in Turkish. According to some accounts, our conquering ancestors found Turkish-speaking families here. Presumably they gave this name to the locality. In the Middle Ages, the district was chosen by Serbians who had fled from the Balkans as a place favourable for business and trade. Old engravings show mosques and slender minarets among the small houses of the Tabán, proving that a number of Turks also found their homes here. The one-storeyed houses surrounded by high walls, steep roofs, and narrow windows looking on to the street also suggest Turkish origin.

In the eighteenth century the development of the quarter was stalled, partly because Pest had taken over as the main centre of trade. The Tabán's attraction was reduced to its history, picturesqueness and Romanticism. The curving streets and lanes, the old one-storeyed houses, and the poverty of the tenements dug into the earth on the steeper slopes made the place a favourite spot for lovers, artists and romantics, though the taverns and famous old restaurants attracted even the well-to-do segments of society.

In the 1930s the Tabán was almost completely demolished, a loss that the romantics of today still mourn. Its narrow winding lanes made communication with the newly-developed parts of the city difficult and its lack of any sewage system presented a health hazard. Presumably, the destruction of the old quarter seemed easier than reconstruction. Now the district is a park, and only the parish church of the baroque period and a few Classicist and late baroque houses surrounding it survive.

Viziváros (the Water Town), parallel to the Danube and located along the axis of Fő (Main) Street, was once the quarter of the well-to-do bourgeois and trading strata, and is an interesting part of the old city of Buda. Several architectural periods are represented in Fő Street, but it is the baroque that predominates. What lends particular interest to the street is that the quarter used to be called 'the fishermen's town' in the baroque period. This flavour has been preserved in the street names – Fisherman Street and Carp Street – and in the fish restaurants. Batthyány Square, half way down Fő Street, used to be the centre and market place of Viziváros. With its two lovely baroque churches and fine baroque houses, it is the capital's only surviving baroque square. Now, however, little remains of the one-storey houses that made up the old Viziváros.

Krisztinaváros is located to the north-west of the Tabán. This is the most densely built up part of Buda. In the 1920s, there were mainly one-storeyed buildings here. Most of the six-storeyed houses were built in the 1930s and 1940s. The Vérmező (Field of Blood) used to be military grounds until World War II, surrounded by riding avenues. Later it was laid out as a park. Next to the Vérmező lies the Southern railway station. After its destruction during the war it was reconstructed in the early 1960s with an airy, floating ticket hall.

Lágymányos

Lágymányos is the area south of Gellért Hill, bordered by the Danube, Budaörs and the Vienna railway line. Construction of blocks of flats around courtyards was begun on a large scale during the inter-war period. The district was developed in the 1930s into a garden city. Gellért Square and the surrounding streets were completed shortly before the Great War, and the Hotel Gellért was opened during the war itself. The square draws its atmosphere from different sources: from the trams and buses coming from Pest and other parts of Buda, from the guests of the Hotel Gellért and its swimming pool, and also from the students of the nearby Technical University and its hostels. The small restaurants, cinema, department stores and smaller shops on Bartók Béla Street produce a bustling image. This character is even stronger around Fehérvári Street, where there stands a large department store and market. In the area there are also major health centres and a number of ecclesiastical institutions. In the 1960s the Feneketlen (Bottomless) Lake and its surroundings were constructed and this is now a site for walks and sports activities. The building of the Hotel Flamenco was a major addition, broadening the services the district can offer. Móricz Zsigmond Circus and Kosztolányi Dezső Square are also big junctions. One of the capital's new housing estates was built here between 1956 and 1964.

The Inner City

The term 'Inner City' used to refer to the inner core of the city within the medieval walls, and to Lipótváros to the north. In present-day usage it is applied to a far larger territory, including the present Fifth District within the Small Boulevard but stretching out across the Grand Boulevard to Arena Road. Now even the inner parts of Buda are often considered to belong to it.

The real core of Pest can be found in the northern part of the Inner City, where the city divides into two: into the world of offices and banks, and into the shopping centre, where shoppers crowd the colourful streets. There is also a great difference between the north and south of the city. Its southern half does not have the same throbbing vitality, being quieter as well as more neglected. Its characteristic features are the University of Economics, the Market Hall, and the newly-built Hotel Korona. This part of the inner city took on a secondary role in the eighteenth century: craftsmen and less wealthy artisans lived here, along with Serbians, Greeks and gypsies in a locality full of inns and so-called 'houses of ill repute'. The northern half had a different character. The specialized shops of the tradesmen were well respected by the local population. There were shops selling ironware, china, stationery, jewellery and books, as well as beer houses, cafés and small boarding houses, which combined to produce a lively social and business life.

In the 1820s, the city began to expand over the old walls. The city gates and walls were demolished, opening the way for development and modernization. The direction of development was set by the main roads leading out from the old city gates. At first it was the southern part of the city which developed faster. A district of retailers, artisans and crafts-men grew up there. To the north, development occurred along Király (King) Street. Sugar (Radial) Avenue was designed to relieve the crowded district of Terézváros (Theresa Town), and to link the inner city with City Park, expressly developed to offer recreation and leisure to the people.

In 1821, Pest was the centre of the political reform movements. The Reform Age was not only full of the objectives of political and national independence, but also of new trends in architecture. The protests of the burghers against the absolutism and anti-Hungarian policy of Francis I, who ruled from 1792 to 1835, gave birth to Hungarian Classicism, which reflected primarily Italian and French elements, to which German elements were subordinated. This trend rejected the use of more valuable materials, such as stone facing, partly for ideological (anti-aristocratic) reasons but also out of economic considerations, preferring brick walls and plastered façades instead. The simple building materials and method of construction they used, together with particular features, such as façade proportions, combined to produce a Hungarian style different from the Classicism of other countries. The Classicism of Pest is characterized by pilasters clasping two storeys, with a central portion ornamented with columns or pillars. It was most commonly used in the apartment blocks of the period, but public buildings and even palaces were also built in this style. Only later did it appear in ecclesiastical architecture, when the Hungarian Protestants used it in their churches to express their opposition to the Catholic Habsburg imperial house. Yet Classicism did not win universal approval. Count István Széchenyi, who was one of the major figures of the Hungarian Reform Age, saw medieval Gothic as the architectural style best suited to the Hungarian landscape and environment.

Some of the finest examples of Classicism from this period were built in Lipótváros in the early nineteenth century. Lipótváros lies to the north of the Inner City and was the first part of the city which was built in a consistent style according to a master plan. In the spirit of Classicism, the district is a network of streets crossing at right angles, parallel and perpendicular to the Danube. Unfortunately the Classicist palaces of the southern part of the district were pulled down, and barely a quarter of them have survived. The row of houses built along the

THE CASTLE AREA AND THE RELATED PARTS OF THE CITY

Figure 3.2   The Royal Palace of the Buda Castle

Figure 3.3   The burgher settlement of the Castle district

Figure 3.4 Street on the slopes of Castle Hill.
View of Viziváros

Figure 3.5 The northern and eastern slopes of Castle Hill: Viziváros below the
Matthias Church and Hotel Hilton

THE INNER CITY

Figure 3.6   The bank of the Danube River at
Pest and the Inner City

Figure 3.7   The Inner City: Károlyi Mihály Street

Figure 3.8 View of a street in the Inner City: Kossuth Lajos Street

Figure 3.9 The Clotild Palaces at the junction of Kossuth Lajos and Váci Streets. The Elizabeth Bridge in the background

The urban environment

Figure 3.10 The centre of the Inner City: Vörösmarty Square and the Gerbeaud (confectioner's) building

Figure 3.11 The Lipótváros (Leopold Town): the governmental quarter and the Parliament

Figure 3.12 Hősök (Heroes') Square: the Millennial Memorial, the Museum of Fine Arts and the Exhibitions Hall. The Castle of Vajdahunyad

Figure 3.13 Blaha Lujza Square: the junction of the Grand Boulevard and Rákóczi Street

Figure 3.14 A recently-built condominium in the part of Lipót City fast becoming a slum

Figure 3.15 Nagydiófa Street: detail of the rehabilitation of a block of flats in the outer part of the Inner City

OLD BUDA

Figure 3.16 Traditional environment of Old Buda: Kolosy Square

BUDA HILLS

Figure 3.17 Gül-Baba Street: the Rózsadomb

Figure 3.18 Semi-detached houses along Törökvész Street on the Rózsadomb

Figure 3.19 Rózsadomb: private villa in the Endrődi Sándor Street

THE NEW HOUSING ESTATES OF THE CITY

Figure 3.20 One of the housing estates of the inner zone: the housing estate of Old Buda: the neighbourhood of the Flórián Square Flyover Bridge. The Margaret Island in the background

Figure 3.21 The housing estate of Ujpalota in the outer suburban zone

Danube near the city, and the Ritz, Hungaria and Bristol Hotels which were all destroyed during World War II, were true masterpieces of Classicism.

The period before the Compromise, the 1850s and 1860s, were characterized by Romanticism and subsequently by early Eclecticism, although Classicism continued to feature. In Pest the main objective of Romanticism was the creation of a national architecture. Its most outstanding products are the Vigadó (Concert Hall) with its elegant façade overlooking the Danube. This served as the *petit bourgeois* casino, hosting the balls, concerts and different festivities of the burghers. The building of the Hungarian Academy of Sciences is also a product of early Eclecticism, as are the Basilica (the largest Catholic church in Pest), the public baths on Margit Island, and the synagogue on Dohány Street. The three-to-four-storeyed palaces and apartment blocks on Sugar (Radial) Avenue were also built in this style. This avenue, now known as Andrássy Avenue, is one of the most beautiful streets of the capital. Almost half way down the avenue lies the neo-Renaissance Opera. The avenue leads out to Heroes' Square in front of the City Park. The square is dominated by Millennial Memorial, built in 1896 to commemorate the millennium of the Hungarian Conquest, and is flanked by the Museum of Fine Arts to the left, and the Palace of Exhibitions to the right. Both museums were built in the style of the Italian Renaissance. The construction of Sugar Avenue was completed in 1887. At the same time the Public Works Committee decided upon the construction of the Grand Boulevard (Nagykörút). The inner ring road, the Small Boulevard, had already been completed, though it had yet to be paved and have trees planted. The Grand Boulevard stretching from Margit Bridge to Petőfi Bridge, can be broken into four arcs. It is architecturally relatively monotonous, in the sense that there are few squares or public buildings along it. However, the uniformity is relieved by a number of valuable architectural creations: the early Eclecticism of the Vígszínház Theatre with its Renaissance elements, the cast iron Western railway station displaying elements of Romanticism, the surviving Classicist houses down Király Street flanking the passages to the Jewish quarter, the art nouveau palace of the Academy of Music, and the monumental New York Palace.

Today's visitor can learn a great deal about the city by setting out to explore the area around the boulevards. Of course, much has changed since their construction. But the districts next to Grand Boulevard still retain their various characters. Going from north to south, the first arc is the most elegant. There are numerous expensive small shops amidst the mostly six-storeyed blocks containing large flats and roof terraces; there are numerous good restaurants, beer houses and cafés, expensive cars are parked in the streets, and the people are elegantly dressed. The second and third arcs are even busier. The traffic is heavier because of the nearby railway stations and the shops. Here the shops are less elegant, and their goods are cheaper. The Grand Boulevard itself is in good condition, but the buildings immediately behind it badly need restoring after many years of neglect. The streets and small squares further away are somewhat quieter with few shops and less crowds. Here we find fewer cars parked, and they tend to be of cheaper makes and in worse condition. Yet the ageing four- and five-storeyed buildings are capable of springing surprises, with beautiful features such as friezes, ornaments, decorated windows and gates. Reaching the fourth arc, the streets have a small-town atmosphere, with smaller, even one-storeyed, buildings hidden among the larger ones.

This tour along the Grand Boulevard reveals both how differentiated the various parts of the city are, and how the demands made upon architecture have changed as bourgeois development has proceeded. In contrast to the aristocracy of earlier ages, the bourgeoisie, and in particular the *grand bourgeoisie*, took less direct interest in architecture, and preferred to leave the planning and building of their houses to professional architects. The greater demand for and commissions of architects also served to promote the technical development of architecture. Expansion was ensured by the abolition of the system of guilds in 1859 which had guaranteed the monopoly of working craftsmen. This opened up the way for the development of the architectural profession.

The years between the Compromise and the turn of the century were unambiguously the age of Eclecticism, which was the architecture of flourishing capitalism. In those days, works appeared in urban architecture which could not be achieved with Classicism. Hungarian Eclecticism and Romanticism were of a European standard. Eclecticism in Budapest spread about a decade later than in the West European countries. Its immediate antecedent was Viennese Eclecticism: the building of the Ring, with its neo-Renaissance blocks of flats, the Viennese Opera, and also the Italian Renaissance universities. The essence of Eclecticism was that each building was erected in a style befitting its role. Hence, Eclecticism was a deliberately pluralist style.

In the last decades of the nineteenth century, the Eclecticism of Budapest entered a new period, that of mature Eclecticism, the quality of which was poorer. This trend corresponds to the late German variant of the style. Baroque and Renaissance motifs were mixed in many buildings. Although Hungarian Eclecticism suffered from a tendency of seeking effects for effect's sake, it could still produce harmonious pieces of art that fitted nicely into their environment. Yet these buildings could not match the grandeur of Paris and Vienna.

The end of the century saw art nouveau enter the architectural scene. This new trend lasted from the millennium until World War I. A group of Hungarian architects, having tired of the stylistic repetitions of

Eclecticism, wanted to make a radical break with the past, with academicalism and the official trends. Art nouveau, which advocated the transformation of the traditional Eclectic forms, and which stood for functionalism, offered the chance to make this break. And it quickly brought considerable success. The Academy of Music on Liszt Ferenc Square was built in this style, as were the Clotild palaces on Felszabadulás Square, which were commissioned by a female member of the ruling Habsburg house. The Hotel Gellért and its swimming pool, the Drechsler palace, the Pension Institute of the Hungarian State Railways opposite the Opera, and the Gresham palace, overlooking the Danube on Roosevelt Square, are other examples of this style.

The movement's success was established by the fact that a significant variant of the innovative movement also evolved: the so-called 'Hungarian art nouveau'. Young architects created a special national style out of the international language of forms and the elements of Hungarian folk art. They also stressed the difference between Hungarian architecture, and of Budapest in particular, and the Austrian, mainly Viennese, architecture.

The movement looked for motifs to the descendants of the Aryan peoples who had migrated to India with the Hungarians from their common Asian homeland, but the search extended only as far as the late-sixteenth-century Indo-Islamic components. These historical elements were combined with Hungarian folk motifs.

In 1879 the Museum of Applied Arts was inaugurated in the presence of the Hungarian King. The building is perhaps the best example of Hungarian art nouveau. The ceramic ornamentation of the high roof, the oriental atmosphere of the sills, and its bright colours and playful elegance mean not only a break from the greyness of the age, but also a bold challenge to the dominant trends in architecture. This is reflected in a number of Hungarian art nouveau buildings, such as the Geological Institute in Népstadion Street, the Post Office Savings Bank which today houses the National Bank on Hold Street, the National Institute of the Blind in Ajtósi Dürer Row, the Budapest Zoo, the Gutenberg Palace, and the arcaded bazaar on Dohány Street. Other examples include the Rózsavölgyi house on Servita Square, the grammar school in Abonyi Street, the charity hostel in Amerikai Street, and the school of commerce in Vas Street.

In the early 1900s this trend was pushed into the background, when it turned out that the popular motifs in themselves were insufficient for the realization of functional and monumental works. Hungarian architectural opinion is still divided in its assessment of art nouveau. Many people hold the view that the individualistic buildings broke up the image of the city and are in glaring contrast to their environment, producing a sense of the unfinished. The turrets, wooden structures and domes seem to be unjustified. Others believe they provide interesting and colourful highlights to the city.

The country-town atmosphere of the old city completely disappeared with the construction work carried out after the Compromise. Planning disrupted the meandering inner squares and streets with its geometric principles. Shops lost their local character, as the share of their customers from the local population declined. The flavour of old small-town life is only preserved in two promenades, Váci Street and the embankment of the Danube. The tourists flooding the modern hotels along the river and people taking the air have finally given the district a throbbing metropolitan atmosphere.

The huge multi-storeyed buildings of the Intercontinental, Hyatt and Forum Hotels, unabashed examples of modern architecture, are the source of much architectural dispute. The criticism is made that they do not fit in with their mostly Classicist environment and that they cut off the Inner City from the Danube.

The Pest bank of the Danube extends beyond the old core of the city, and includes other parts of the present-day Inner City. The governmental quarter was developed in the northern part of Lipótváros (Leopold Town) in the late nineteenth century. Its most significant building is the Parliament, built in an Eclectic, neo-Gothic style. The square around it is occupied by grand buildings containing ministries and offices, giving the quarter a busy feel in the daytime, but leaving it quiet in the evenings.

The Pest and Buda sides of the Inner City are linked by bridges that are famed for their beauty. Margit (Margaret) Bridge is the northernmost bridge, meeting the northern end of the Grand Boulevard. To the south lies the favourite of the local inhabitants, the Chain Bridge, with its evening floodlights and fine arches, which stands as a tribute to the Reform Age city- and bridge-builder, Count Széchenyi. The bridge links the northern end of the Small Boulevard with Clark Adam Square. Here stands the Zero Stone, the point from which all Hungarian road distances are measured. Leading off from the square to the right is Fő Street, which heads up through the Viziváros to Batthyány Square. Straight ahead is the tunnel under the Castle Hill, taking traffic from Pest through to Krisztinaváros in Buda. At the southern end of the Small Boulevard the Szabadság (Freedom) Bridge (or Franz Joseph Bridge, as it was known before the war) leads to Kelenföld, Lágymányos and the southern slope of Gellért Hill in Buda. The southernmost bridge of the Inner City is Petőfi Bridge. The Grand Boulevard crosses the river and continues round on the Buda side through Moszkva (Moscow) Square to the Margit Bridge. The middle of the five bridges is the Erzsébet (Elizabeth) Bridge which is an extension of Rákóczi and Kossuth Lajos Streets. At the time of its construction (between 1897 and 1903), it was the largest single-arched bridge in Europe and the most beautiful suspension bridge in the world. Like all the Budapest bridges, it suffered the fate of being blown up by the retreating Germans in 1945. The new Elizabeth Bridge, which was opened in 1964, is in many ways similar to the original, and shows German and English architectural influences.

When admiring the bridges, one notices the baths and swimming pools along the Buda side. Near the Buda bridgehead of the Margit Bridge are the Császár (Emperor) and Lukács (Luke) baths and the Komjádi swimming pool. Nearby at the northern end of Fő Street are the Király (King) baths, and at the Buda end of Elizabeth Bridge there are the Rudas baths, the Imre baths, and a little further from the river bank, the Rácz baths. Facing Szabadság (Freedom) Bridge there are the Gellért baths, within the wonderful building of the Gellért Hotel. Swimming pools and baths can be found in Margaret Island, such as the baths of the medicinal Hotel Thermal, the Palatinus open air swimming pools, and the National Sports Pool. Nor is the Pest side devoid of baths. In the City Park there are the Széchenyi baths, which like all the others are fed by medicinal spas. There are also baths outside the Inner City; the Dagály swimming pool lies at the Pest end of Árpád Bridge, and there are baths at Római Fürdő, Csillaghegy and Pünkösdfürdő on the Buda side, and at Pesterzsébet in Pest.

These swimming pools and baths attract local and foreign visitors not only for their curative properties, but also for their architecture. From the Árpád dynasty onwards, many historical eras have erected baths in recognition of the healing power of spas, spawning architecture to suit these needs (Szviezsényi, 1939). Sadly, neither their waters nor their architecture have been adequately protected. It is particularly the Turkish baths that are in danger now, and are in desperate need of repair. However, the Gellért and the Széchenyi baths have recently undergone reconstruction work. The new and elegant medicinal Hotel Thermal was built in place of the medicinal bath designed by Miklós Ybl, which was destroyed during World War II.

Walking through the Buda side of the Inner City from north to south there are several localities that deserve mention. Mártírok útja (the Road of Martyrs), for instance, which is the continuation of the Grand Boulevard of Pest on the Buda side, borders the Viziváros, forming part of Buda's outer boulevard. Around the Mechwart Gardens stand several public institutions, including the district council, and the Central Statistical Office. Moszkva Square is situated at the crossroads of Mártírok útja, Krisztina Körút, and Szilágyi Erzsébet Avenue, which leads out to Buda Hills. This square has seen many uses. When its mines were filled in after World War I, it was turned into tennis courts, and now is a major transport terminal, serving trams and buses and the metro. During weekdays it is crowded with people going in to work, and at weekends, many people change here on their way out to the hills for excursions. Next to Moszkva Square is Széna Square (Haymarket), where a coach terminal and a number of commercial establishments can be found. Near Széna Square stands the Fény Street Market, famous for its flower market, but also offering a rich choice of vegetables.

Óbuda (Old Buda)

The old settlement that dated back to the Romans on the plain between the hills and the Danube was totally destroyed during the Turkish period. After the expulsion of the Turks it became the property of the Count Zichy family. From the eighteenth century onwards it was a royal estate, mainly belonging to the Queen. The inhabitants were engaged in agriculture, viniculture and milling in almost total seclusion. To some extent this seclusion survived even its merger into Budapest. The range of the József Mountains stretching to the Danube has always separated Óbuda from Buda proper, and transport links with Pest are not easy.

Óbuda first developed in a modest baroque style. Rural single-storeyed houses with narrow façades and long courtyards stretching behind were built in the zigzagging streets. In the early nineteenth century, when the *embourgeoisement* of the population was proceeding vigorously, the more ornamented late baroque and Classicist houses lent a new character to the neighbourhood. During the period after the Compromise, the development of Óbuda lagged behind the rest of the capital. It lost its earlier baroque atmosphere and became increasingly rural.

The outer regions of Óbuda did not suffer this setback in development. Besides the detached family houses built on the northern slopes of the Ferenc Hill, another settlement which developed along the Roman bank has been important in offering popular recreation facilities for water sports. The Roman remains at Aquincum, excavated in the 1880s and 1890s, represent a major attraction for tourists.

From the middle of the twentieth century the architectural environment of Óbuda changed completely. Old districts were pulled down to make room for new housing estates, a large shopping centre, and the road heading toward Szentendre, although efforts were made to retain the more valuable sections and buildings. This included the main square and the streets leading off it, the Classicist building of the district council, several pleasant houses of the period, and the former Zichy palace. Preserving the memory of earlier architecture are the main parish church of Óbuda, the synagogue, and the Protestant church of Kálvin Street. In the basement of one house a museum was set up presenting the Roman camp. The oval-shaped building of the silk-spinning workshop near Árpád Bridge, built in Louis XVI style, is a true monument to the age of Joseph II (1780–1790). The restoration movement of the late 1980s has undertaken the rescue of this and other old buildings. This is important, as Óbuda holds a special place in the hearts of the capital's inhabitants for the small taverns, restaurants and old neighbourhoods that have an atmosphere of their own.

The Buda Hills

The Buda Hills have a local colour that is special to Budapest. The long slopes have been favourable for agriculture, especially for viticulture, until around the Compromise. It subsequently became a popular site for recreation and home-building. Construction began in the 1840s and 1860s, as the intelligentsia and the richer inhabitants of Pest built their Classicist and Romantic villas. Until World War I it was mainly summer houses that were built, but during the inter-war period an increasing number of permanent residences appeared. This has long been a prestigious residential area of the city.

In the 1960s private construction began in the area, financed by investments that were strictly controlled and assisted by the state. The better educated, skilled classes with credit and capital who had not benefited from the state's housing policy started to build semi-detached houses in this area. The belt of semi-detached houses that appeared has grown in intensity, and the plots have become smaller. The architectural character of the area is quite varied. There are family villas built in the Classicist and Romanticist styles after the Compromise, and family houses built by the emergent *grand bourgeois* strata in the 1970s and 1980s: two- or three-storeyed buildings in modern, post-modern or even in Classicist style. Several public institutions have also been built here; big children's homes, laboratories, and research institutes. Here and there are clusters of taller buildings. The greenery, the quiet, the clean air, and the long stretches of forest have made the residential areas of Zugliget, Hűvösvölgy, Pasarét, Németvölgy, around the Budakeszi road, and even on the Rózsadomb in the inner part of Buda favourite spots of excursions out from Budapest.

Twentieth-century housing developments

Viewing the city from Gellért Hill, one can see that the capital is surrounded by two rings of new estates. The first ring is attached to the inner parts of the city, and can be found in the suburbs of the so-called transit belt, while the second ring is located in the formerly autonomous suburbs.

Modern architecture made its appearance in Hungarian urban design in the first decade of the twentieth century. At that time the pure uniform forms and the potential of reinforced concrete and glass enjoyed only a limited appeal. Nor were the city authorities any more receptive. Advocates of modern architecture could construct only a few public buildings on account of their leftist leanings. These included several schools and churches. However, modern apartment blocks became fashionable because of the functional demands of the bourgeois strata. Examples of the Modernist style are the modern blocks of small flats that were built at Pasarét in 1931. This was the start of the construction of modern family houses in Budapest, primarily among reform-minded intellectuals. In the early 1940s, two large working-class housing estates consisting of detached houses were built, one in Angyalföld and the other one at Albertfalva. They were financed by the Social Security Fund.

Up until 1951, only a few apartment blocks and experimental small housing estates of 7–800 flats each were developed. Traditional materials were usually used and the construction was similarly traditional: no departures were made from the existing street plan or system of plots. In keeping with the architectural ideology of the period, modern architectural forms were rejected by the advocates of 'socialist-realism' and those who wanted to revive the so-called progressive national traditions. One reason was the fact that the building industry, which had been nationalized in the early 1950s, was not equipped for the manufacture of the structures that modern architecture required, and no opportunities for importing were available.

Socialist-realist architecture developed in the Soviet Union in the 1930s. After the war its purpose was to serve the highly centralized management of society in the East European countries. It was a fundamentally ideological style of architecture, detached from real social needs, which sought to express the strength and greatness of the working class by architectural means. The public buildings were almost monumental, decorated with friezes representing scenes from workers' lives. In this style, Classicist and Eclectic forms evoking national traditions were gradually enriched by art nouveau elements. The Thälmann Street housing estate of Angyalföld and the estate at Béke Square in Csepel are examples of this style.

Only in the 1960s and 1970s did the mass construction of housing estates begin. In this period, larger housing estates of 2,000 flats were built in the outskirts in place of demolished residential areas in industrial districts. The housing estate of Lágymányos was one such development. Originally the idea was to build blocks of the same height around closed, or almost closed, courtyards, but over time the design became less compact. Some of the buildings are symmetrical, but there are also long rows of buildings running perpendicular to the street, and tower blocks

49

as well. The largest housing estate of the period, which consisted of 7,500 flats, was built between 1958 and 1965, and lies in the newly-developed outer Ferencváros on the Üllői Road. But here it was not the street plan that determined the design, but the conception that the estate should be broken up into neighbourhood units. The housing estates of the 1960s kept to the traditional design of basing the layout on the street plan, and using traditional materials.

Kelenföld was a pre-World War II industrial development on the flat land between the Vienna railway line and Albertfalva. It is a mixed development, where from 1965 onwards long ten-storeyed rows and tower blocks were built in the midst of factories, tenement blocks, villas and smaller detached family houses. A similar estate with rows of uniform buildings is being built in Kőbánya, the oldest industrial district of Budapest.

By the 1970s a huge system of investment and construction had emerged capable of building more than 10,000 flats in an estate. It developed standardized identical buildings using the prefabricated technology of house factories, laying down increasingly restricted standards. These estates were located in the suburban districts of Budapest, either in what used to be separate villages or in newly developed areas. Examples of the latter include Kispest, Budafok, Rákospalota, Békásmegyer, Újpest, and later Gazdagrét and Káposztásmegyer.

The developments built in the 1960s and 1970s have increasingly lost any individual architectural character. The Eclectic elements have been abandoned, and the new solutions are monotonous in both their architecture and their layout. The buildings are constructed using prefabricated blocks made in housing factories, and a high proportion of them stand over nine storeys high. It is against the interests of the large state investment companies to build lasting structures that are costlier to maintain, particularly when their sole target is quantity, which pushes all consideration of quality into the background. Essential services such as crèches, kindergartens and schools are either missing or are insufficient. The development of open spaces, parks and playgrounds is usually poor.

The old suburbs

Very little of the old suburbs survive: partly because – as we have seen – new housing estates were built in their place, and partly because the inhabitants themselves have transformed them with new family houses. But they were also transformed by the redevelopment of their centres. In most suburbs new centres with public offices, childcare institutions and other services have been developed. Yet some parts still retain the old rural atmosphere. Cinkota and the outer parts of the Rákos suburbs retain something of their pasts. Most of the villages that were formerly separate from Budapest – Rákosszentmihály, Mátyásföld, Sashalom, Pesthidegkút and Csillaghegy – consist mostly of detached family houses with small gardens. One can find here the continuity of construction that is common to many small Hungarian towns. Rákospalota is one such example. And although life is naturally entirely different here from in the capital, and sometimes more difficult, yet it holds a growing attraction for many. The detached houses with gardens and fresh air, offering opportunities for cultivation, are increasingly in demand. Nor are the transport facilities too bad, offering easy access to workplaces and shops in the city centre.

Part Two

City dwellers

4
The people of Budapest

The demographic processes in a city are a good reflection of its economic situation and role within its sphere of influence. Demographic changes in capital cities also indicate the condition of the broader country, and Budapest is no exception. The Hungarian capital serves as a barometer of the entire process of Hungarian urbanization. This is due to two factors: (1) the city has had a prominent role in the Hungarian urban network in respect of its population, as well as in its space organization functions during the entire modern period; (2) Budapest has been the first to absorb new phases and forms of European urbanization and has spread them more or less successfully within the Hungarian settlement network. Budapest has been the first to reflect new phases in the development of the Hungarian society. Therefore, any explanation of the demographic situation of the capital derives not merely from its internal conditions, but much more so from the economic and social condition of the country and its place within Europe.

The characterization of demographic conditions is a complex matter. Economic growth was only one factor attracting immigrants: those seeking safety in the aftermath of World War II also gravitated to Budapest. Natural change, meanwhile, reflects health conditions (such as the level of infant mortality), the cultural level of the population, popular attitudes to the family and to birth control, and so forth.

The growth of population and its sources

In 1869, the last census before the 1872 merger of the three cities of Buda, Pest and Óbuda, presented their total population as 280,000, and that of the outer belt (which was incorporated into the capital in 1950) was 22,000. Only 1.8 per cent of the country's 15.5 million population lived in the capital. In terms of size, the city ranked seventeenth among European cities.

Since then there has been continuous population growth – disregarding the decline during World War II – right up to 1970. In the 1970s population growth came to a halt and the number of inhabitants stabilized at around 2 million. At the time of the 1990 census, the number of inhabitants was 2,016,000, 2.1 per cent less than the population in 1980. However, with the population of the country as a whole falling by 3.1 per cent, the proportion living in Budapest has risen to 19.8 per cent. Growth has been fed mainly by internal migration during the past 100 years. Natural growth has always been low, even during the period when the age structure of the population was young. Rural immigrants have rapidly adapted themselves to the urban demographic custom of having small families. In this they were assisted by the tradition of family planning practised by certain sectors of the Hungarian rural population to prevent the fragmentation of holdings. (Under Hungarian inheritance law, land has to be distributed equally among the children who inherit it.)

Population growth was fastest between 1872 and 1910, after the creation of a united Budapest. This was the major period of Hungarian industrial expansion. In one decade alone (1890–1900) the population of the city grew by 45 per cent. In 1900, 861,000 people lived in the area of the present city (733,000 within the 1872 boundaries). By 1910, this figure had risen by a further quarter of a million, making Budapest one of the few European cities with more than 1 million inhabitants. (In 1910, it was the eighth biggest city in Europe in terms of population.) And the process of suburbanization had already begun. While the population of the city grew three times between 1869 and 1910, that of the outer belt grew tenfold.

At the turn of the century the city was very young as a result of constant immigration. 38 per cent of its population was below the age of 20, and only 5 per cent was over 60. Natural growth was also relatively high, at 10 per 1,000 population, but quite low in comparison to the Hungarian countryside and to other East Central European cities. During the first twenty years of this century natural growth contributed only 130,000 people to the 1 million inhabitants of the city, while immigrants accounted for 240,000 of the growth of these years.

The turn of the century was a critical period for Hungarian agriculture. It was struggling with problems of overproduction, the latifundia were dominant, and there was significant overpopulation. Yet even though many people left the countryside, Budapest was able to avoid the overpopulation common in big cities in developing countries.

A considerable proportion of the rural migrants left the country and went mainly to North America. And the majority of those who came to the city were absorbed by rapidly-expanding industry and by large-scale construction activities. There was also room for the immigrants, as many flats were being built at this time, for the most part one-bedroom flats with the most basic facilities. In the early twentieth century, the municipal council and some large companies built up-to-date workers' housing estates too, on the principle of the English 'garden city'.

The population growth of the inter-war period was shaped more by the crisis of the city than by the boom of the capital. The population grew by a little over 200,000 between 1920 and 1941, a growth which was almost exclusively accounted for by in-migration. After 1930, there was a natural decline: deaths outstripped births by 9,400 between 1931 and 1941.

As a consequence of the Versailles Peace Treaty after World War I, the country lost two-thirds of its former territory. Consequently, Budapest's sphere of attraction shrunk radically, and its earlier functions were reduced. The city's dominance became disproportionately great within the territory that remained, and as the country's only large city it continued to grow during the inter-war period. In 1920, 15.5 per cent, and in 1941 18.3 per cent of Hungary's population lived in the capital. (A similarly critical period was experienced by Vienna, the 'number one city' of the collapsed Austro-Hungarian monarchy.) After the disappearance of the unified market of the monarchy, Budapest's economy entered into a long period of recession. In-migrants could find work only with difficulty, unemployment became massive (especially around the years 1920 and 1930), and slum developments emerged as the number of those unable to find accommodation grew.

In-migration was nurtured by two main sources. One was the exodus of the Hungarian population from territories transferred to other countries by the peace treaty. A large proportion of the people who left their homes were intellectuals employed in the former Hungarian public administration, education and cultural life, for whom it was particularly difficult to find employment. The in-migrants played a significant role in the anti-semitic wave from the 1920s onwards as they tried to get jobs by squeezing out the Jewish intelligentsia, who had a major role in Budapest. (In 1920, about half of the physicians and lawyers in Budapest were Jewish.)

The other large group of immigrants continued to come from the over-populated agricultural sector. The land reform of the 1920s did not significantly alter the dominance of the latifundia, and the extremely conservative Hungarian government was in the hands of the aristocracy. One-third of the agricultural population had no land whatsoever, and as the opportunities for emigration ceased, they looked for jobs inside the

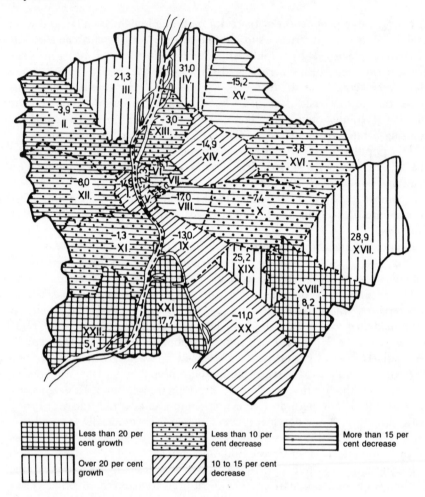

Figure 4.1 Population changes (1980–1990)

country, migrating from one place to another. Thus it is understandable that many tried their luck in the country's only big city.

World War II, which was the biggest crisis the city had hitherto suffered, brought rapid growth for some years. This was again due to refugees. The population of the city reached the 2 million figure for the first time in March 1944, and one year later the census recorded about 1,400,000 inhabitants among the ruins.

The fifteen years after World War II brought about the last significant population growth: the number of inhabitants grew by more than 400,000 between 1945 and 1960. Growth continued at a slow pace for another decade or so, until the population stabilized at around 2 million, showing occasional modest growth. The last vigorous wave of growth was the result of the dynamic industrial development of the 1950s, when in-migrants were attracted by the new industrial jobs. In 1964, the city's industry employed more than 700,000 people, half of the country's total industrial employment. At that time it was the biggest industrial centre in East Central Europe. The management of the nationalized economy was also concentrated in the capital.

There has been little change in the number of inhabitants during the past two decades. Natural decrease has persisted (1980/90: − 4.7 per cent), which in-migration can no longer offset. The radical fall in in-migration is due partly to the vigorous industrialization of the agricultural regions, and partly to the small numbers in the younger age groups leaving the countryside. (Natural decrease has become a general phenomenon all over the country.) From the 1970s attempts were made to stem in-migration to Budapest by administrative measures (one had to live or work in Budapest for a minimum of five years before acquiring the right to apply for a socially distributed flat, or for favourable credit to build one). But this had little impact (at most it speeded up suburbanization), as there have always been jobs available in abundance in the capital. What it did do was to swell the numbers living in workers' hostels or as lodgers.

In-migrants and out-migrants

Migration has been the major factor accounting for Budapest's population growth in this century. Few of these in-migrants have come from abroad, as there were only limited legal means (by marriage or the uniting of families) for this. And they for the most part came from the Hungarian minority of Romania. Two big groups of in-migrants came from the countryside: workers (mostly unskilled) coming from the backward, especially the north-eastern parts of the country, and intelligentsia from every part of the country, but mainly from the university cities.

During the inter-war period – despite the economic depression – the capital was the only market in the country absorbing labour to any degree. Between 1920 and 1930, 130,000 new jobs were created in Budapest compared to the 42,000 created in the rest of the country, although the difference in the number of the young entering and the old leaving the active workforce was 900,000 outside Budapest. A huge, redundant labour force accumulated, mainly in the agricultural regions of the Great Plain. In the 1930s, the development of the war industry in the country offered 60 per cent of the new jobs. But the number of in-migrants coming to the capital exceeded the number of new jobs by an annual average of 20 to 30 per cent between 1920 and 1940. During these two decades, a large stratum of the poor accumulated in the city. The in-migration of workers has dropped since the 1960s, while that of white-collar and service sector employees has been increasing. A highly qualified intelligentsia is strongly concentrated in the capital: 75 per cent of those employed in the Hungarian R&D sector are located here!

There has also been constant out-migration from Budapest: to the country towns, to the settlements of the surrounding agglomeration, and abroad. No exact data are available for the last group, but it cannot be insignificant. Estimates put the figure at 4–5,000 people annually, most of them highly qualified. The winter of 1956–7 was a special period when – after the defeat of the revolution of 1956 – about 100,000 Budapest inhabitants fled to the West. The growing European (and world economic) integration of Hungary will obviously strengthen the process of international migration. Foreign capital and international companies come primarily to Budapest. Since 1988 Hungarian citizens have been free to undertake jobs abroad and their stay abroad is not limited.

The capital receives in-migrants from every county in the country, but the largest numbers come from Borsod-Abaúj-Zemplén and Szabolcs-Szatmár counties in the north-east. These two regions are very different from each other: the former is a depressed heavy industrial and mining region, where there has been considerable unemployment resulting from industrial restructuring; the latter (the only county showing natural population growth) is still an overpopulated agricultural area.

The city of the aged

The fall in the birth rate over recent decades and the drying up of the in-migration of the young have resulted in the ageing of the population. Almost a quarter of Budapest's inhabitants are over 60. With the retirement age at 60 for men and 55 for women, and with the real value of pensions declining rapidly due to inflation, this represents a considerable section of the population living in worsening financial conditions, and squeezed out of society. The old residential quarters near the city centre are increasingly becoming slums, partly as a consequence of this shameful impoverishment of the old. The middle classes are staying in the inner parts of the city as they get older and poorer, and as they die, it is for the most part the marginal groups in society that are moving in.

The process of ageing can be expected to continue, as is indicated by the fact that the proportion of the younger age groups below the age of 20 is of the same size as that of the groups above 60. In 1987 there were only 9.3 live births per 1,000 inhabitants, the lowest since demographic records began. The number of live births (19,555) was hardly higher than the number of abortions! If natural miscarriages are also considered (3,490), less than half of the embryos were born. The high mortality rate (14.1 per 1,000) started to fall after the shocking growth from the mid-1970s onwards. (The peak was reached at 15.1 per 1,000 in 1980.) In the 1980s, an average of 10,000 more people died than were born in the capital. The mortality of the middle-aged male population has been particularly conspicuous. One-fifth of men between the age of 55 and 59 died, and this is double the proportion for women in the same age group.

Ageing has further demographic consequences. As life expectancy is much higher for women than for men, there is a considerable surplus of women. Only one-third of the 215,000 inhabitants above the age of 70 are men (73,000). A surplus of men is only found among age groups up to the age of 30.

The decrease in the number and proportion of marriages is partly a consequence of ageing: whereas in 1973 there were 22,000 marriages in the capital (11.1 per 1,000 inhabitants), this figure was only 12,700 (6.1 per 1,000) in 1987. However, the low proportion of marriages is not only the consequence of the age composition of the population. Several signs indicate that the traditional family is in crisis. The high proportion of abortions is one, and another is the number of divorces. In 1987, 7,900 divorces were declared by the law courts, and there were 622 divorces per 1,000 marriages. This proportion has almost doubled during the past fifteen years, and the trend has grown particularly steeply in the 1980s. In 1987, 20,500 marriages were terminated by divorce and death, whereas there were only 12,700 new marriages; this represents a fall in the number of marriages of almost 8,000. A 'marriage deficit' has also been rapidly growing: in 1977 it was only 1,300.

At the other end of the age structure, infant mortality has fallen significantly (44.6 per 1,000 in 1971 and 18.3 per 1,000 in 1987), although this is above the national average.

The leading cause of mortality – as in most European countries – are diseases of the circulatory system which in 1987 accounted for 15,000 out of the total of 29,000 deaths. (7,000 people died of heart disease.) Malignant diseases come second, accounting for 7,500, followed by death through violent causes (accidents, suicides) at 2,400 (1987 figures).

Summing up, the demographic condition of the capital reflects the poor quality of life. Health conditions are poor (high mortality rates), as is public morality (high rates of divorce and abortions). The same is true for Hungary as a whole, and the demographic situation of some rural regions is even worse than that of the capital. However, demographic conditions are better in the majority of Hungarian cities, ageing is more moderate, and the proportion of people of active working age and the birth rate are both higher.

The geographical distribution of the population

The demographic centre of gravity of the capital shifted from the city centre to the outlying districts long ago, as is generally the case in larger modern cities. This process has largely been directed by the property market (prices in the city centre have become so prohibitively expensive that properties cannot be used for housing). This has been going on for the past forty years, in spite of the fact that the property market officially ceased to exist. The modern city has been undergoing structural change, the spontaneous processes of which have been mediated by different mechanisms. The utilization of space in a city has a rationality according to which each part is favourable for different functions. It is a common-place that the institutions visited by a large number of clients and exercising authority are located in the city centre, and this is dictated by the rationality of access and of political culture. Although the institutions and the mechanisms mediating rationality are significantly different in market economies from those of the state socialist command economies, the results are nonetheless similar. This phenomenon is analysed in greater detail in Part Three of this volume.

One of the rare essays written in English about the Hungarian capital (Beynon, 1943, pp. 256–75) described this phenomenon almost fifty years ago. The inner parts of the city, namely the present governmental and shopping centre of Pest, and the Castle area and its neighbourhood in Buda, already had an annual population decrease of about 2 per cent between 1880 and 1935. Within this period, between 1920 and 1935, the decrease of the population extended over the densely-populated inner residential belts embracing the historic city centre.

After World War II the large housing estates were built far from the city centre, mostly beyond the pre-1950 city borders. Nevertheless, the inner residential belts have not been depleted, despite the constant decrease of the population, and the residential functions of the city centre have remained significant. Few office buildings were built in the Central Business District. Under socialism, the bodies of government that managed the economy took over the property that had served as banks, company headquarters and even flats. The population decrease of the inner residential belt is closely related to the ageing of the population.

Between 1980 and 1990 the population decreased in fifteen of the twenty-two districts of Budapest, and fell by 15 to 17 per cent of its earlier size in the inner districts. Half, or in some places even more, of this decrease was the result of emigration, but not of natural decline. In the seven districts showing population growth, there was also a natural decrease, and any increase was due exclusively to in-migration. In four districts the population has grown by more than 20 per cent within ten years; the growth was the largest in the Fourth District (the northern part of Pest), reaching 31 per cent, in which probably the very last large housing estate of the capital is being built at Káposztásmegyer with 30,000 inhabitants already. Thus, the 1980s have brought about a significant transfer of the population. However, the most populous districts (six districts have more than 100,000 inhabitants each) are not yet the most peripheral ones, but the outer districts of pre-1950 Budapest.

5
The urban society

The development of modern bourgeois society

The organizing forces of political power

The modern urban society of Budapest was shaped by the same forces that transformed the three cities into one capital and subsequently into a metropolis. The axes of power have changed over time according to the different social groups present within or attracted to the capital. The formation of society brought some groups to the centre of social, political and economic life, while moving others out to the periphery.

In Chapter 6, which deals with housing, we consider in greater detail how, after the expulsion of the Turks, power considerations and Austrian imperial settlement policy influenced the social composition of Pest and Buda from the late seventeenth century onwards. This was partly through representatives of the imperial public administration and of the army who settled mainly in Buda, squeezing out others, or at least making the inflow of the Hungarian small nobility from the counties more difficult. The policy of restricting citizenship to Hungarians and Catholics mainly affected the tradesmen and craftsmen who were seeking to come to Budapest. Those of non-Hungarian nationality were given plots of land for houses entirely, or almost entirely, free of charge and were exempted from paying taxes for several years.

It was mostly Austrians, Germans, Catholics and Hungarian aristocrats and members of the gentry who lived in Buda. Hungarians of lower social status, and people of other nationalities and of religions other than Roman Catholicism moved mainly to Pest. The followers of Calvin and the Jews were banished to Óbuda by administrative measures.

This settlement policy had a different effect on each of the societies of the three cities: not only in that Buda was an aristocratic and Pest was a bourgeois city of traders, but also that their relationship to central authority and to the main social and economic forces of the age was also different. Buda was a settlement faithful to feudal society and to the emperor; Pest was a city that was tolerated but that could not be dispensed with, inhabited by those who were squeezed out of both Buda society, and of the focus of power.

The organizing force of capitalist development

The gradual unfolding of capitalist social and economic organization soon transformed the hierarchical order of the cities. Pest, which had flourished as a city of merchants in the early sixteenth century, enjoyed a revival after 1686. Due to its favourable geographic location and the existing road network, industries related to agriculture began to develop first, particularly those with commercial links such as the processing of tobacco. By the middle of the 1800s Pest was the centre of national transport, and a trading centre (especially for grain), the cradle of the engineering industry that developed out of the milling industry, and the centre of banking. As a result of these processes at work, the significance of Buda decreased while that of Pest rose.

The beginnings of modern urban society

In the period following the expulsion of the Turks, the society of Buda seems to have been relatively constant. Its structure was balanced and homogeneous. The proportion of the bourgeoisie was high, although the number of the very wealthy within that class was relatively small; Pest offered opportunities for rapid enrichment but also for impoverishment.

For those engaged in industry, membership of a guild was essential. In Pest a number of industrial guilds were established under the supervision of Vienna. Hungarian craftsmen of various industries, together with their foreign masters who settled here, were all under German leadership. Many people came from Austria, and it was at this time that a number of Serbians moved to Pest. 'These foreigners constituted the backbone of the bourgeoisie of Pest, of that middle class that was becoming wealthy through industry. They did not bring an elite patrician past with them, or a special, time-honoured social status, but rather the simple essence of industrial work' (Dümmerth, 1968, p. 61). The bourgeois development of the city was mainly determined by the fresh approach and management of the socially almost homogeneous German and Austrian *petit bourgeois* and middle bourgeois strata of the towns.

Another major component of the bourgeoisie was the Hungarian artisans moving in from the agricultural market towns of the Great Plain: the tailors, button makers and boot makers. These in-migrants already had urban or even often bourgeois backgrounds. The gentry that later achieved the status of the patricians and burghers came from the royal free towns. Those who came from the villages were the former poor serfs who had been liberated from the devastation of Turkish rule and were looking to escape from that state of dependence. They engaged in transportation and day labour in the service of the better-off citizens. Their situation was rather difficult, as they had neither houses nor land of their own. They were excluded from the privileges of urban citizens, since only those who had a house or land qualified as such. Very few could rise from the state of serf to even the lowest rank of urban society.

Differentiation rapidly took place among the merchant classes. Some of them rose to the wealthiest patrician strata of the city dominated by Germans. There were also ambitious elite craftsmen to be found among richer groups. Soon they appeared in the bodies of local government beside the earlier professional bureaucrats and the intelligentsia. The way into the middle classes was, for Germans, mainly through skilled crafts, and for the Hungarians, through transport and commercial catering. To some extent this occurred independently of Austrian settlement policy, being the outcome of the needs of daily social and economic life. This would explain why Hungarians dominated in this sphere.

The integration of the nationalities

These processes gradually transformed the hierarchical order of the different nationalities which so marked the relationship between Buda and Pest. The framework of the existing hierarchy could be broken by inherited social rank in Buda, and by wealth and ethnic origin in Pest: just as the Hungarian aristocracy was let into the upper social circles of Austrians and Germans in Buda, so the Hungarian merchant and elite craftsman of Pest gained access through the wealth they acquired to the German-dominated group of merchants and craftsmen. Which was quite natural, since the hierarchy of nationalities concealed a hierarchical social order: the proportion of patricians, public officials, and *grand* and middle *bourgeoisie* was higher among the Germans, while that of the *petit bourgeoisie* and the poorer plebeians was higher among the Hungarians.

Gradually, as Hungarianization spread, German dominance was reduced to the control of power. The integration of the different nationalities took place on the necessary basis of the shared community.

The Hungarianization noted by contemporaries was only partly the outcome of the growing proportion of Hungarians. It was also due to the growing assimilation of the Germans and Slovaks in the city. The strong Hungarianization taking place among Jewish families was also significant. Statistics published in the 1850s tried to hide the transformation that had taken place in the relationships between nationalities: the proportion of Germans was repeatedly raised arbitrarily to the detriment of Hungarians and other nationalities, trying to offer numerical justification for the ethnic basis of power relations.

According to the 1851 census, the proportion of Hungarians in Buda was almost 17 per cent, and over 33 per cent in Pest (Spira–Vörös, 1978, p. 239). More than 60 per cent of the inhabitants of Buda had German as their mother-tongue. In Pest this figure was 33 per cent. Almost 3 per cent of the inhabitants in Buda were Slovaks, and a little over 4 per cent in Pest. Serbians constituted 2.5 per cent in Buda, and 0.6 per cent in Pest. The numbers of Romanians and Croatians were very small. By the merger of the three cities in 1872, the proportion of Hungarians had further decreased (Spira–Vörös, 1978, p. 240). In 1870 the proportion of Hungarians had reached 46 per cent, and the other nationalities constituted 54 per cent. In 1880 Hungarians constituted almost 57 per cent of urban society, Germans 34 per cent, and other nationalities about 9 per cent. In 1890 the Hungarian share approached 68 per cent, and Germans nearly 15 per cent. During the twentieth century the Hungarian share of the population continued to rise: in 1900 it was 80 per cent, in 1910 86 per cent, in 1920 almost 90 per cent, in 1930 94 per cent, in 1941 96.6 per cent and by 1949 it had stabilized at around 99 per cent. More than 20 per cent of the population of the capital was Jewish, the majority of whom declared themselves Hungarian at the censuses. Unlike elsewhere in Eastern Europe, the Jews were a religious rather than an ethnic group because of their rapid assimilation.

Social stratification

By 1872 a radical social and economic differentiation had taken place among the citizens of Pest, which saw the beginning of the evolution of the different groups that made up the modern *grand bourgeoisie*. Their number was still small, around 1,000 families only. Fewer than 500 of these could be counted as rich. Some were merchants, manufacturers and bankers coming from the country or abroad, who had a considerable amount of capital, and who wanted to invest in enterprises. Those members of the earlier *grand bourgeoisie* who had their wealth safe in real estate and houses now availed themselves of the new economic opportunities offered by new enterprises. Others were afraid of change, and by keeping a distance from the hub of the economic life, became isolated. Many went into public administration and the professions. They expanded the numbers of the Buda and Pest intelligentsia, for example, by joining the growing circle of increasingly famous doctors and lawyers. It was the merchants who were best able to retain their position among the old *grand bourgeoisie* through trade and the manufacture of wine, tobacco and wool. By the second half of the nineteenth century trade had become completely transformed, though, as the earlier Balkan connections were replaced by the western market. Foreign textiles, handicrafts and fashion goods, citrus fruits and spices were traded to produce an increasing amount of capital. The significance of trade in cereals and cattle also grew, especially among the respectable merchants coming from the country.

An increasing number of aristocratic families appeared among the *grand bourgeoisie*, who used their profitable real estate and other property to become entrepreneurs. Over time they came to dominate the boards of the urban limited companies and the Commission of Public Works, and it was they who handled the merger of the three cities. After 1867 and the end of absolutism, the liberal aristocracy withdrew from urban public life, and had to yield control to the new *grand bourgeoisie*. However, they were still active in the economic life of the capital, at the head of credit institutions and insurance companies. In contrast the old, more traditional *grand bourgeoisie* could not keep up with the new processes, partly because of the fragmentation of wealth through inheritance, and they were pushed into the background and gradually isolated.

By this time the *grand bourgeoisie* dominated, by commerce and increasingly by property ownership and the independent manufacturing industry. Their desire for status created a great fashion out of noble titles. They were also keen to participate in political life on the basis of their increased economic weight. This modern, internally diverse *grand bourgeoisie* was united in its basic interests, but sharply differentiated in terms of family ties, residence and daily human contacts.

Social polarization created groups within not only the *grand bourgeoisie*, but also the peripherally positioned masses of the *petit bourgeoisie*. The crumbling barriers of the guild system also made independent operations theoretically possible within small-scale industry and the retail trade. The age of Absolutism (1849–67) abolished the requirement of licences issued by the guilds, but retained their professional control. This was how the guilds tried to limit the growing independence of new groups, particularly of the Jews. They had little success. The number of in-migrants grew constantly. By 1870, only 482 of the 2,372 shoemakers of Pest were born in the city (Spira–Vörös, 1978, p. 227). Many leading master craftsmen wanted to end the limitations of guilds, and a surge of social groups flooded Pest from all over the country, all hoping to establish themselves independently. There was a major rise in the number of clerks and employees with secondary education because of the needs of the bourgeois state, the demand for expertise, and the increasingly complex administrative and economic functions of the city.

The demand for retail trades and catering saw a growth in the number of tobacconists, pubs, cafés and inns. In 1870, 3,500 independent merchants and small restaurants were recorded. Some of the retail merchants were able to accumulate capital, but many made only marginal profits, satisfying the demands of the poorer strata. This shows that it was only in part the enrichment of the city that shaped the *petit bourgeoisie*. Equally important were the desire for upward mobility and an escape from poverty.

In the middle of the 1800s the *petit bourgeoisie* stratum numbered 35,000, while by 1870 this figure stood at around 55,000. In Buda the *petit bourgeoisie* cannot easily be separated out, since they were interwoven with workers and white-collar employees. In 1914 their number was 128,000 in Pest and Buda together. Their number was swelled from three sources: those who wanted to escape from poverty, those who wanted an independent existence, and the growing number of state employees. The 1848 Franchise Act expanded the numbers of the enfranchised: it abolished the category of 'citizen of a royal free borough', and introduced property-related criteria expressed in terms of taxes, or a corresponding degree of education. The only sections excluded from citizenship now were the plebeian strata, such as the non-elite workers, servants and day labourers.

The evolution of the working class

From the middle of the 1880s the emergence of the urban proletariat was most significant in the structural transformation of the society. In 1857, 50,000, and by 1870 97,000 people were seeking employment on the labour market. In Pest, industry and catering employed 33,000 qualified workers. In Buda there were 4,500 skilled workers. According to 1870 data there were 21,000 people living on unqualified, casual work for daily wages and there were about 20,000 servants. There were approximately 2,000 day labourers and 3,000 journeymen in Buda, and data survive about more than 2,000 servants. The shipyard and textile mill of Óbuda employed 2,500 workers. Óbuda also had 8,000 agricultural labourers and 4,000 servants and day labourers. Of the 270,000 inhabitants of the three cities, almost one-third belonged to these three categories (Spira–Vörös, 1978, p. 232).

Their number grew because of the rapid development of large-scale industry from the 1850s onwards. But the domestic supply of labour posed problems. Austrian and Czech competition drained the supply of local skilled and semi-skilled workers who could operate machines. Therefore, the demand for labour in the new large-scale industries was partly met by foreigners. Workers came mainly from the German-speaking provinces of the monarchy, taking a 20 per cent share in the metal industry workforce, and a 40 per cent share in engineering industry. Their proportion was negligible in small-scale industry.

During the 1860s and 1870s, workers gradually polarized according to income levels, housing conditions, and also on the basis of industrial traditions. Skilled workers with a better income could rent a flat of their own more easily in the inner parts of the city, or build houses in the outlying districts, and they could have their children educated. The workers coming from the northern parts of Hungary, for the most part Slovaks, were, with their mining and lumbering backgrounds, better able to integrate into industrial labour and urban conditions, than those coming from the south, especially those coming from the Great Plain.

In 1890 the working class already constituted almost 40 per cent of the urban population. More than 51 per cent of the nearly 237,000 manual workers were employed in industry; most of them were found in large-scale industry, as the proportion of wage labourers in small enterprises was less significant. Among skilled workers, a high-earning elite emerged. The position of foreman appeared, particularly in the transport and manufacturing industry. The proportion of unskilled workers, servants and day labourers was constantly decreasing. Some joined the industrial workforce as semi-skilled labourers. After the turn of the century there were already 337,000 workers in Budapest. Most were skilled, and had an income higher than the national average for workers. A large proportion of them were young, and the number of women among them was growing.

The social stratification of the modern bourgeois city

At the turn of the century Budapest had a typical capitalist development structure. Its modern urban society consisted of many strata: *grand*, middle and *petit bourgeoisie*, white-collar employees and intellectuals, and a working class. By then Budapest had become the fully developed economic, administrative and communications centre of the country. However, the social groups living in so-called respectable poverty, even if not in complete destitution, appeared in greater numbers in Budapest than in the major cities of the more advanced Western European countries. The large-scale opportunities for enrichment were now limited, and it was hard even for those who enjoyed economic independence to escape from poverty or break out from the *petit bourgeoisie* into a higher level of the social hierarchy. Too many people were waiting at the door of middle-class existence hoping for admission. Besides those who enjoyed some independent economic existence, we also find the lower ranks of the state and economic bureaucracy – the clerks, lower white-collar workers, teachers – and also some better-skilled groups of workers who had higher incomes. There were public transport employees, who had a modest but guaranteed livelihood: the elite manual workers, the foremen and the junior officers. Of this crowd gathered at the threshold of bourgeois life, many stepped back rather than forwards during these years. Small enterprises and retail traders went bankrupt in massive numbers as a result of the economic depression of the twenties and thirties.

Entry into the middle classes was possible only where large industrial and financial capital had little interest. Opportunities were better in the catering and retail trades, in some peripheral parts of transport such as the haulage business, and in the smaller branches of industry concentrated in limited companies. The middle strata of the bourgeoisie, which were weak both in number and in capital, formed an increasingly closed group. After the turn of the century the number of economically independent entrepreneurs among them decreased, and the majority tended to be professionals, and middle- and higher-level bureaucrats in public administration with good incomes and property. In the meantime, huge wealth accumulated in the hands of a narrow layer of about 500 *grand bourgeois* entrepreneurial capitalists, national leaders and professionals, mainly through property, credit, manufacturing and building industries and transport.

Table 5.1 presents the social structure of the 1920s, emphasizing the extremely low proportion of the upper and middle classes, and the high proportion of the *petit bourgeoisie*, and of the workers in particular.

In the inter-war period, grave social, economic and political crises sharpened the main features of the social structure that had developed by the turn of the century, to become even more marked. The number of manual workers grew, while the middle strata continued to shrink as a result of an internal structural transformation that saw the number of economically independent people decrease and the proportion of white-collar workers, salaried state officials and intellectuals grow (see Table 5.2).

By the early 1940s, urban society was strongly differentiated. Differentiation was not only present among the major social groups and classes, but also within the individual groups: a narrow elite had evolved everywhere, with varying levels of wealth and integration into the main axes of society. The past and the future divided metropolitan society in a way that was typical of East Central Europe. The development of

City dwellers

Table 5.1 The strata and classes of Budapest society in 1919 (per cent)

	Budapest	Suburbs	Greater Budapest
Upper ruling and leading classes	2	1	2
Middle classes	10	5	8
Petit-bourgeoisie	28	20	25
Workers	60	74	65
Total	100	100	100

Source: Horváth, M., 1980, *Budapest története* (The history of Budapest), Vol. 5. Akadémiai Könyvkiadó, Budapest.

Table 5.2 Active earners by employment in Budapest (per cent)

	Budapest		Suburbs		Greater Budapest	
	1930	1940	1930	1940	1930	1940
Independent	21.0	14.1	18.7	12.1	20.4	13.6
Blue-collar workers	59.6	62.4	71.1	75.8	62.6	66.1
White-collar employees	19.4	23.5	10.2	12.1	17.0	20.3
Total	100.0	100.0	100.0	100.0	100.0	100.0

Source: Horváth, M., 1980, *Budapest története* (The history of Budapest), Vol. 5. Akadémiai Könyvkiadó, Budapest.

urban society constantly reflected its feudal past, even as the bourgeois framework took shape. Practically all of the social groups in this capitalist development had feudal roots. In the sometimes dichotomous values of the nobility and the bourgeoisie, the values of tradition, descent, inherited rights and property, and the exclusivity of the Estates, were mixed with the values of enterprise, diligence, democracy and openness.

In the brief and hardly harmonious coexistence of past and future, the curious duality of the old bourgeois strata, with their feudal roots, and the new strata marked the entire social structure for a very long time. This dual structure was an involuntary compromise between the weakened feudal system and the bourgeois system that was not yet strong enough. And it reflected the main features of East Central European social development: it was based on the inadequate weight of the middle classes and on the dominance of the *petit bourgeoisie* and the poor. The ruling strata of the past and the future were forced to strike a bargain because of the lack of capital, and to seek common protection against the masses that were excluded from bourgeois advantages.

Similar, though not identical, bargains were struck during the bourgeois development of West European countries, but were quickly dissolved after the consolidation of the bourgeois order. This dissolution took place organically, on the basis of the regularities of capitalist development, and of the relationships of wealth and economic power. Such was not the case in Hungary.

With the appearance of state socialism, the dual social structure and its characteristic urban society was temporarily pushed behind the scenes. It disappeared without any chances of dissolving the earlier historical bargain, or of reaching new compromises. Perhaps it will get the chance now, with the establishment of democracy at the end of the twentieth century. This new agreement will partly depend on the nature of the urban society inherited from state socialism.

Urban society under state socialism

The shaping force of the redistributive mechanisms

The constructive role of the state has historically been strong in Hungary. Even before World War II, the state's activities substituted for the accumulation of capital based on internal development; industrial growth unfolded as a result of the banking system because of the limitations of capitalist development. State interference in the private economy was frequent during the pre-war capitalist period, too. Unlike the general trend in the developed world, the institutions of the state continued to determine the social structure. The relations of the feudal social structure, which were closely incorporated into the activities of the state, did not allow for the separation of state and civil society that characterized bourgeois societies.

The economic crisis between 1945 and 1948 further strengthened state interference prior to the Communist takeover. It reached its height under state socialist rule, when the separation of society and state almost completely disappeared. The state penetrated into practically all spheres of society: the economy, political institutions, and even into people's daily lives. And it began to reorder the existing stratification of society. The class structure of capitalists and wage labourers was wound up by the transformation of property relations and the elimination of private property, by land reform and by the subsequent collectivization of agriculture.

The institutionalization of the state's restructuring role had grown to an unprecedented extent as state control was extended over social and economic resources. By the 1960s, a highly centralized state-political control developed to regulate the production and distribution of the socially produced surplus. Only subsequently did certain social groups and the decentralized state and political institutions begin to assert a form of control (Kolosi, 1983, p. 89).

The redistributive mechanisms founded under state socialism significantly affected the structure that emerged (Szelényi, 1990, p. 203). Social groups were integrated differently, since they were differentiated, and the old lines of power were broken as new groups emerged in the processes of social reproduction. Nevertheless, the redistributive mechanisms could not entirely eliminate the earlier structure, nor totally define the newly evolving social stratification. This was partly because, despite all their efforts, the difference between the political state and civil society could not be totally eliminated. Some forces of society resisted the state's desire to penetrate every sphere of life. The former medium and *petit bourgeois* strata, the intellectuals and the pre-war elite retained civic values as well as material wealth. These groups were ready to take advantage of the revived market conditions and establish the so-called 'second economy'.

In the 1960s the Hungarian Communist leadership was willing to integrate certain mechanisms of the market economy – the relationships of commodities and money – for the sake of the intensive development of the economy. Some degree of commodity production, economic rationality, and decentralized decision-making was introduced into the processes of redistribution. Consequently, the hitherto illegal civil society re-emerged and flourished. In the countryside it was mostly in the form of part-time farming and house-building. In the cities, it meant the building of flats, various kinds of overtime, and goods acquired by supplementary income. The limited accumulation of capital – quasi-*embourgeoisement* – began outside the sphere of state redistribution. The more skilled and educated workers, white-collar employees and junior intellectuals acquired the income and housing conditions of the *petit bourgeoisie* and the middle class.

Thus the gentry-bourgeois dual structure of the pre-World War II period was replaced by another dual structure: a social articulation shaped by redistributive and market mechanisms. For a while the market mechanisms corrected the social inequalities deriving from state redistribution, but then they started to create new ones, strengthening the earlier inequalities as well (Szelényi, 1990, p. 203). Other dichotomous mechanisms were also at work, for example, the unequal significance of urban and rural settlements, which further differentiated the structure of the society (Kolosi, 1983, p. 95).

The major features of the social structure

The social structure which had developed by the turn of the century was modified in a number of ways after 1949. The number of blue-collar workers stopped growing, and their proportion of the total society began

Table 5.3 Changes in the structure of active earners by type of employment (per cent)

	Blue-collar workers	White-collar workers	Independent employees
1941	60.4	23.4	16.2
1949	63.4	22.5	14.1
1960	67.6	28.6	3.8
1970	54.9	42.9	2.2
1980	50.4	47.6	2.0

Sources: Census Data of 1941, 1949, 1960, 1970 and 1980. Central Statistical Office, Budapest.

Table 5.4 Distribution of blue-collar workers by qualification (per cent)

	Skilled workers	Semi-skilled workers	Unskilled workers
1960	40.7	29.0	30.3
1970	44.6	30.9	24.5
1980	50.6	36.6	12.8

Sources: Census data of 1960, 1970, and 1980. Central Statistical Office, Budapest.

to fall, although they continued to represent the most significant group in society. The economically independent were forced out and their numbers fell sharply after 1960. The proportion of white-collar workers and intellectuals rose consistently during the same period (Table 5.3).

From the mid-seventies onwards, changes took place amongst blue-collar workers. The distribution of workers by branches of industry changed, and the overall proportion of industrial workers fell. The numbers employed grew more rapidly in the building industry than in the service sector. The most significant change took place in the skill structure of blue-collar workers. The proportion of the better trained and semi-skilled workers grew, while the number of unskilled workers fell (see Table 5.4).

The better trained workers increasingly formed a closed group: skilled workers were mainly recruited from their own social stratum. Some enjoyed upward mobility and became direct production managers or technical intellectuals. However, from the late sixties, upward social mobility became increasingly difficult. Unskilled workers without educational qualifications could only become semi-skilled workers, and only a small number could rise to the level of skilled workers. Some semi-skilled workers managed to become skilled ones, while others became unskilled office workers. Women joining the ranks of blue-collar industrial workers appeared in larger proportions in the less qualified occupations.

City dwellers

Sociological research has shown that skills continued to be the main factor in the differentiations among blue-collar workers even in the latter part of the 1980s. Education and differences in types of secondary school graduation had less significance in the variations in living conditions (Kolosi, 1983, p. 123). More skilled workers were also more easily admitted into urban society. A large proportion of less skilled workers lived in the agglomeration surrounding the city. They had to suffer the difficulties of commuting, were squeezed not only out of professionalization and school education, but also out of state housing and subsidies on urban public services.

The development of the new power elite and the intelligentsia

The privileged position of the pre-war ruling class was quickly broken, and then eliminated within the state socialist structure. Administrative measures and political resettlements removed a considerable part of the middle class from the capital, and many of them, particularly among the *grand bourgeoisie*, left not only the city but the country as well. The factories, shops and flats of both those who stayed on, and those who left, were confiscated. Other measures were also taken to strike at the former *grand* and middle *bourgeoisie*: they could not get important jobs and their children were not admitted to the universities.

In keeping with its ideological objectives, the new power elite and the political and economic bureaucracy was built by the representatives of the working and peasant classes that had been in a disadvantaged position in the capitalist system. The nationalized enterprises, the different offices of public administration and ministries were directed by managers and officials from working-class and peasant backgrounds. In the country as a whole, almost 90 per cent of the political leaders and 65 to 70 per cent of economic managers had blue-collar backgrounds. In Budapest the proportion of those who had a working-class background was somewhat lower, but the trend was the same (Kolosi, 1983, p. 123).

The intelligentsia was not created by state socialist development, but by broader historical processes. Although the intellectuals had been incorporated into the earlier bourgeois society, they remained distinct on account of their different backgrounds and wealth, as well for the different values and ideologies they professed. They contained groups with links to the nobility and to the bourgeoisie, to the locality and to cosmopolitanism, to the peasantry and to the workers. After the elimination of this earlier class articulation within the intelligentsia, they appeared as an autonomous social stratum (Kolosi, 1983, p. 131). The state socialist policy of equalization brought a considerable change in their position, and their living conditions sharply deteriorated. But they

Table 5.5 The composition of intellectuals by social position of father and by place of residence between 1961 and 1964 (per cent)

Social position of father	Budapest	Intellectuals Country town	Village
Leader and intellectual	25	21	16
Other intellectual	16	18	15
Craftsman	13	18	11
Skilled worker	22	18	10
Semi-skilled worker	3	3	2
Unskilled worker	8	4	6
Agricultural blue-collar worker	13	18	40
Total	100	100	100

Source: Andorka, R., 1982, *A társadalmi mobilitás változásai Magyarországon* (Changes in social mobility in Hungary), Gondolat Könyvkiadó, Budapest.

were also hit by the general anti-intellectual policy of the period. But even this was far from straightforward: at first it was apparently directed only against those bourgeois intellectuals who had acquired privileges in the pre-war society. Steps were also taken towards the creation of a new, so-called 'socialist intelligentsia'. Talented workers and peasants were taken out of their environment and were sent to school, and their children were given beneficial access to university.

Social mobility research shows that the proportion of people from working-class backgrounds showed a sharp increase among leaders and white-collar workers living in the countryside. As Table 5.5 shows, the proportion of those with backgrounds as leaders, intellectuals and skilled workers was highest among the Budapest intelligentsia in the early sixties. From the mid-1960s onwards, Budapest, like other towns, saw a decline in the presence of those of working-class origin, indicating the increasingly closed nature of the stratum.

From this period onwards, the new tasks of the intelligentsia integrated them more closely into the reproduction of the social structure. Their role was now to maintain expertise and economic rationality in management. They also mediated between different social interests and the centre's expectations and opportunities. In many respects this brought an improvement in the situation of the intellectual groups. Yet there were inconsistencies in terms of their position in the division of labour, in their qualifications and income, and consumption and lifestyles (Kolosi, 1984, p. 208). These inconsistencies show the peculiar relationship between the intelligentsia and the authorities, and the limited opportunities for social participation.

The disputes of the seventies concerning the social position of the intelligentsia made it clear to the political leadership that this stratum was less and less inclined to accept a position that was financially unfavourable compared to that of their Western European counterparts, or even that of earlier generations. The political leadership accepted the need to improve the financial position of the intelligentsia, but did not want to achieve this at the cost of a change in the distribution of power or to concede a critical or oppositional role in a liberated civil society. The answer lay in the second economy.

The restructuring function of the second economy

Research during the eighties has made it clear that, in spite of the major significance of the second economy, it had a negligible impact upon social stratification. Almost everybody had the opportunity of making additional income to compensate to some extent for the disadvantages of social origin, and to increase material well-being. But it was a way of increasing income, rather than a means of changing one's place in the social structure. Positions in the division of labour and place of residence continue to have a stronger influence on the differences in culture and lifestyle and in the material conditions of life (Kolosi, 1984, p. 208).

Nevertheless, the experiences of the 1970s and 1980s also show that the wealth and income conditions of a section of the intelligentsia were improved through the mechanisms of the quasi-market and the second economy. About 36 per cent of better-off intellectuals participated in the second economy (Kolosi, 1984, p. 208). However, other advantages that derived from the position they occupied in the redistributive structure were at least as important in the improvement in their living conditions as their participation in the second economy. It proves that wealth can be reached by different ways and means, particularly in the case of workers in Budapest. The second economy has had even less effect upon the internal stratification of workers, as the better-off workers could not break out of their income position through the second economy.

The new structural processes and changing urban society

The political changes of the early 1990s and the legal safeguards guaranteeing market relations and enterprises offer a better opportunity for the separation of the state and civil society, and for the emergence of a social structure more typical of modern market economies. The state's role in structural redistribution is declining, while the market is getting stronger.

The reorganized processes of social reproduction are transforming social stratification as well. The earlier pattern of urban stratification is being cut through by new elements: the highly differentiated job and income opportunities of the state and private spheres, and the consequently different structures of consumption, culture and lifestyles. The state sphere also offers diverse opportunities, although it is the bureaucratic elite that benefits rather than the experts, though this may simply be due to the different degrees of integration of the two groups. The situation of intellectuals and other social groups integrated into political institutions through the different political parties is better than that of those who for different reasons have stayed outside: further proof that the system of political institutions is still of structural significance.

It is clear that the development of the market is not an easy process, and will presumably not be a short one either. Some analogies can be found in the social structure that evolved at the turn of the last century. The lack of capital has restricted the development of the middle classes, while the *grand bourgeoisie* has hardly appeared at all. The groups that have slipped down from the quasi-middle strata, for whom state socialism meant a good standard of living, and the well-off skilled workers who have become *petit bourgeois*, are waiting for higher social status, but this wait may prove a long one. It is mainly the mass of semi-skilled and unskilled labourers and unqualified white-collar workers who are slipping downwards in the social hierarchy, and are left out of the increasingly dynamic market sphere. There are various possible scenarios: if there is a large-scale influx of foreign capital and a rapid spread of market relations, not only may the well-off bourgeois strata expand, but there will also be more chance of a social policy that can prevent mass pauperization. However, this would require a more daring concept of entrepreneurship from the state and more vigorous political and legal guarantees of the market mechanisms.

6
Human ecology and the problems of housing

Historical roots

The significance of historical processes

Historical influences, spontaneous social and economic processes and the direct intervention of city planning and politics have all played a role in the development of the spatial social structure of the city, and in the location of the various social groups within the urban area.

The diverse roots of the three original towns, the development around several nuclei and, most of all, the historically different functions of the towns naturally determined their social structure. The more aristocratic structure of medieval Buda and the high proportion of patrician families naturally derived from the fact that it was a royal seat. Pest, on the other hand, the originally mercantile, bourgeois town, was inevitably the home of bourgeois strata. Those engaged in agriculture tended towards Óbuda. The influence of these different centres over the settlement naturally changed over time, but their effect can still be felt: Buda still attracts the elites, and Pest is home to the medium strata of society.

A description of the early history of Buda will give an idea of how this segregation evolved. After the Turkish occupation, the Austrian imperial settlement policy clearly aimed at having a German and Catholic population in Buda and a Hungarian and Serbian one in Pest. Elite Austrian officials, leading officers of the imperial army, and various monastic orders found their homes in the Buda Castle district. By the late 1700s, Hungarian aristocratic families had set up their households there too.

From this period date the distinguished palaces around Dísz Square, known as Fő (Main) Square in those days. In 1800, the Palatine lived here with his court of about 150 people, government officials, clergy and their attendants. The majority of the burghers also lived in the Castle area, in the streets linking Dísz Square with Szentháromság (Holy Trinity) Square, and in Országház Street. The craftsmen, bakers, shoemakers and joiners lived on Úri Street. Fortuna Street, which was then the busiest thoroughfare of the Castle area, was where the blacksmiths, cartwrights and merchants lived.

After the expulsion of the Turks, German craftsmen working on the reconstruction of the Castle settled down in the suburbs of Buda Castle and in Víziváros (Water Town). In line with the settlement policy of Vienna, various nationalities, but in the main Serbians, were located here. 30 per cent of the plots were purchased by the burghers of Buda Castle and by the officials of the Chamber. Víziváros was mainly inhabited by *petit bourgeois* tradesmen and craftsmen. The bourgeois owners of vineyards, who used to be clerks in the Castle, settled down mainly in Krisztinaváros. The poorer Serbian, Croatian, Bosnian and Albanian cultivators, who had been squeezed out of the Castle area and Víziváros, lived in the Tabán.

In the period after the Turkish occupation, Pest was inhabited mainly by Hungarian gentry officers who participated in the liberation of Buda, and some lower-ranking German army officers. At that time, Pest was merely on the periphery of Buda. Later, after 1692, the so-called external authorities, such as the revenue collection authorities, were moved here. The high-ranking officers of the imperial army, the representatives of Austrian public administration, the salt revenue officers, duty officers, the tollmen of bridges and prominent figures in the Hungarian public administration all sought and found accommodation in the central parts of Pest, in the main squares and in the elegant streets of the inner city. Austrian settlement policy had a varying impact on the different social strata. The members of the ruling class were less affected than the bourgeois, mercantile strata, for whom it was far more difficult to come to Pest. The disadvantaged social and national groups clustered together as if seeking protection from others who felt less threatened. The clerks in the German public administration were more dispersed in the best quarter of the city – in those days Fő (Main) Square by the Danube – than their Hungarian counterparts. The same tendencies are found among the merchants, though the Hungarian merchants grouped together more than the public officials. The Serbian merchants bunched even more strongly, suggesting that they were in an even worse position than the Hungarians. The merchants also aimed for the central parts of the city, and those market places further from the Danube, where they occupied good houses radiating off the area. Property and money can lend more rights and break through the hierarchies of nationalities. Some richer Serbs were able to penetrate into parts inhabited by German and Hungarian merchants. And this seems to be a Hungarian speciality: unlike in medieval cities, representatives of the different industries were grouped not according to occupation in Pest, but to their differences in wealth. The richer craftsmen, butchers, masons, and cartwrights lived side by side, while the poorer members of the occupations were also neighbours.

Positioning within local society 'was greatly influenced by the regions linked by the road network and the city gates' (Dümmerth, 1968, p. 44). It was wealth that decided who could have a house by the more important city gates and main roads, and who could open a restaurant or a guesthouse. The gate of the highway leading to Vienna was particularly important for the city. The elite settled in the neighbourhood of the Buda, and later the Vác Gates; those on the next rank lived near the Hatvan Gate, or the Eger Gate as it used to be called. The Water Gate was a port district giving access to the Danube. Here the population was a mixture of Germans, Hungarians and Serbs. Instead of elegant guesthouses, we find taverns and the homes of the poor day-labourers in this district. The fourth gate was the Kecskemét Gate, the meeting point of the roads leading from the Plain. This quarter was dominated by the wattle houses of day-labourers on the periphery of society.

The processes after the Compromise

The planned urban policy of the period of Compromise played a major role in the broad territorial and social processes. The development programme of the Commission of Public Works, the authority directing urban development, set out the principles for the foundation of the segregated territorial system of the city. It laid down the centralized development of the city and its spatial articulation, setting the direction of expansion, earmarking the functions of the different districts, and dividing the city into zones of construction. Its regulations set the purposes of buildings, the size of plots, the height of the houses to be built, and the material for the walls. This was decisive in terms of the processes of segregation. It was at this time that some significant elements of the spatial social structure of the city developed as a consequence of the conscious planning, through the regulatory systems and the involvement of private capital. Differentiated zones with a definite social composition evolved – differentiated in terms of the construction on open land, the function of buildings, the physical characteristics and structure of housing.

The 1870 census of Pest reflects the occupational hierarchy. A far higher proportion of people working in public administration, or in the professions as lawyers, medical doctors and teachers lived in the inner parts of the city and in Lipótváros, than elsewhere. These were the most well-to-do parts of the city. There was a higher proportion of artisans and other *petit bourgeois* occupations in the outer districts, in Terézváros, Józsefváros and Ferencváros. The financial situation of the inhabitants of these parts was somewhat worse. Craftsmen of lower qualifications lived in larger numbers in the outlying districts. They were the poorest layers of society.

However, such a differentiation only gives a broad outline of the hierarchical layout of the society, as the hierarchy broke down within the individual zones because of the enclaves of lower social groups and because of their more dispersed settlements. The first zone of the spatial system that was laid out in concentric rings was the inner city, the centre of the industrial and urban development until the turn of the century. The considerable expansion here transformed the historical kernel as the growth of the residential zones squeezed out trade and commerce. The dynamic building of apartment blocks played an important role in the changes in the inner city. The blocks of flats with courtyard galleries were the product of general property speculation in the Austro-Hungarian monarchy in that period. With regulations setting the size of the plots, developers sought the most rational use of space, and therefore built round the plot on all sides. Ornamental, aristocratic palaces were built facing on to the street, with large flats that included rooms for the housemaids, whereas the flats looking out on to the courtyard consisted only of a room and a kitchen and often had no bathroom or toilet attached. The quality of the flats differed even from floor to floor. The best flats were on the first floor. Thus these houses had a preconceived picture of segregation from the outset. Rich burghers, or even aristocrats, lived in the flats facing on to the street along the bigger streets, whereas the flats looking on to the courtyard were rented by the *petit bourgeoisie*. The flats facing on to the street in the more modest houses at a distance from the main avenues were occupied by the *petit bourgeoisie* and intellectuals, while the courtyard flats were the homes of workers and craftsmen (Csanádi–Ladányi, 1987, p. 94).

The second, so-called transitory zone was the result of expansive development after the turn of the century. The periphery and the industrial districts of pre-1950 Budapest belonged to this zone with the exception of the Buda Hills. This was the territory where entrepreneurial capital and the socially motivated programme of the authorities built family houses and smaller housing estates of more modest quality for unskilled workers. Later on the middle class also built their houses here.

The third zone consisted of the outer districts, which used to be separate suburban settlements before 1950. The 'Rákos' villages, such as

Rákosszentmihály, Rákoskeresztúr, Rákoscsaba, but also the garden cities and more rural parts of Pesterzsébet and Pestszentlőrinc belonged to this zone. It enjoyed dynamic development after the turn of the century as the plots were cheaper here than in the capital, and offered a safe livelihood to the poorer social groups squeezed out of the big city.

Housing problems and processes of segregation

The economy and policy of housing in the 1950s

The spatial and social structure of the city was modified by the housing policies of the 1950s. Hungary adopted the state socialist housing policies that were found in all East European state socialist systems. Its most important feature was that housing was centralized as a responsibility of the state.

The development of controlled housing

The capitalist economy was unable to function without state intervention even already during the inter-war period. Extremely slow industrial development, declining agriculture, the damages suffered in the war, international credit obligations and debts all made state intervention essential. This tradition was utilized by the Communist Party, which also attributed an extremely important role to the state in acquiring and retaining power. An essential element of its programme was a controlled, or command economy: private capital was increasingly restricted, and production and allocation was controlled even in the field of housing, in contrast to the earlier liberal economy. The outcome of this intervention was that the state became the most powerful customer in the market with the orders it placed during the war, and the compensatory purchases it made after the peace treaty. Because of their dependent position, the major banks and manufacturing industries were controlled and subsequently taken over by the state within a few years.

In 1948, mines, power stations and industrial and transport enterprises employing over 100 people were taken over by the state. In 1949, industrial enterprises employing more than ten workers followed suit, and finally all small-scale private industry and trade was eliminated. The next step was the nationalization of housing. All houses consisting of more than six apartments were to be nationalized. This regulation extended over only 37 per cent of privately-owned apartment blocks, as the majority of them had six or less apartments.

Rents were controlled by a regulation of 1946. This, and a government decree of 1948, formed the basis of the Hungarian housing system right up to 1971 (Mónus–Mosonyi, 1978, p. 93). Two rent systems were developed, one for flats built before World War II, and the other for new ones. In the case of old flats the rent depended on the size of the flats, calculated as a certain percentage of the basic rent (50 per cent in the case of a one- or two-room flat, 60 per cent for a four-room one, and 100 per cent for larger flats). The basic rent was three times the amount of the rent in Pengő as on 1 September 1939 ('Pengő' was the Hungarian currency until 1946 when the Forint was introduced). For new flats the rent was calculated by the square metre: 2.10 Forints in the country, and 2.70 Forints in Budapest (Mónus–Mosonyi, 1978, p. 86). The government decree of 1948 stated that the owner of the flats could not terminate the rent of flats contracted for an undefined period of time by a regular notice to quit, except in certain special circumstances.

The state had removed housing from the laws of the market by introducing a controlled housing economy. There was no relationship between the extremely low rents controlled by the state and the quality of the flats. It was an important principle that rent should be a rather modest sum in family consumption (Szelényi–Konrád, 1969, p. 346). Experts say that these rents operated at the greatest loss in the entire world: 'when the new Forint was introduced the stabilization multiplier was 1.25 in the case of rents, compared to an average of 5 to 10' (Mihályi, 1983, p. 78).

Some features of the controlled housing economy had historical roots in Hungary, and are therefore not a specifically socialist phenomenon (Mihályi, 1983, p. 70). The first such measure was introduced in 1916: rents were frozen at their maximum level in 1914–16, and the rights of property owners were restricted. There were major city interests behind this government measure, demanding intervention because of rising inflation and the constant rises in rent. The restrictions were removed only in 1920 because of the resistance of house owners, but were reintroduced in 1943 (Mihályi, 1983, p. 71). Such a restricted housing economy had very adverse consequences in the 1920s and 1930s, and also during the period after World War II. The state organizations in charge of housing neglected most of the flats, and necessary maintenance and reconstruction were not carried out.

The building of houses by private initiative decreased by 50 per cent between 1949 and 1953. Private individuals were gradually prohibited from building flats to rent. The flats were distributed by the state, practically free of charge, in keeping with its egalitarian ideology. Accordingly every family had a right to a modern flat of their own, which was an allocation in kind besides the wages. The state extracted the cost of building and maintaining housing and the infrastructure from wages. Hence, housing ceased to be a commodity.

City dwellers

The building and allocation of flats

The state, or the political authority hidden behind it, had unlimited power over the extent and form of housing in the state socialist model: the population could not influence the supply of flats by any means, either by need or by demand. The state made housing and infrastructure in general a low priority in the interests of forced economic growth and industrial development. A relatively small proportion of investment was spent on housing. Only 1.4 per cent of GNP was spent on housing between 1951 and 1954. In the sixties this figure approached 2 per cent, reaching 2.6 per cent in the seventies (Ekler–Hegedűs–Tomsics, 1980, p. 155).

In the first part of the 1950s few new flats were built because of the emphasis on heavy industry, and up to 1959 over 20 per cent of new houses that were built by the state were in the new industrial towns. It was also clear that in the allocation of housing the main task was to serve the interests of large-scale industries, to supply the manpower necessary to the factories and to assist the establishment of new industries. The politically important cadres enjoyed advantages all over the country. Housing became one of the most important means of reward. The big flats of those who died, were interned or who emigrated were also allocated along similar lines in Budapest.

At an ideological level the democratic nature, or at least the labour class characteristics of the allocation of flats, was stressed: that is, that the socio-political objective of the housing model was to eliminate differences in the housing situations of families. No reference was made to the housing problem of the people in rural areas, who constituted 55 per cent of the Hungarian population at that time.

Changes in the economy and politics of housing: the dual system of flat allocation

Masses of people left the villages and agriculture to seek out the opportunities offered by so-called socialist industrial development. They went to the new towns and to the capital to seek jobs and accommodation. This brought on a considerable housing shortage. By the late 1950s, it had become clear that the increasingly grave housing problem could no longer be kept secret and that some new response was needed. People would not accept purely ideological arguments, and their faith in the housing allocation policy of the state, projected as an egalitarian one, was shaken. New elements were continuously introduced to the housing economy, initially by the crisis of the early 1950s in the monolithic political system based on the authority of a single individual, then by the

1956 revolution, and finally by the political and state authority that took shape in the new political consensus. It was decided that the housing shortage should be ended and that private construction should be encouraged, together with a market operating under state control.

The government approved a fifteen-year housing plan in 1960. The programme, which promised fundamental improvements in housing, was aimed at the elimination of the 'quantitative housing shortage'. This concept was invented to lay the foundations of standardized flat building that aimed only at the growth in the number of flats. It completely disregarded differentiated social and family needs, concentrating on an abstract notion of families in need of housing. The resolution laid down that 1 million new flats were to be built by 1975, of which 600,000 were to be owned by the state and 400,000 by individuals. It also ruled that the flats owned by the state were to be built primarily in settlements inhabited by workers in the capital and in the large provincial towns. It was laid down in the programme that the majority of flats, with all amenities, were to be built in housing estates with basic public utilities and green spaces. The fifteen-year housing programme was achieved, and even exceeded by 5 per cent.

The second fifteen-year plan was passed for the period between 1976 and 1990. Besides considerations of quantitative development, the programme also stipulated so-called qualitative requirements to achieve a more differentiated structure of flats. The concept of qualitative requirements was intended to introduce quasi-market elements and express some social expectations. 70 to 75 per cent of the 1,200,000 flats were to be built by involving private capital. 315–320,000 flats were to be built in Budapest and in the agglomeration, and another 500–600,000 flats in the other cities. According to the plan, 80 to 85 per cent of the flats were to be built in new housing estates in multi-storey prefabricated blocks.

Each housing programme shows that a limited quasi-market under strong state control was emerging alongside the housing economy of the state authorities. The first element in this change was that people who were given a flat made a contribution to the cost of building according to their social circumstances, number of children and income. Subsequently the state gradually involved the population and even employers in housing through long-term loans and various socio-political discounts.

The authorities kept private construction under rigorous control, partly through state subsidies and partly through different kinds of credit. Support for private construction depended upon the social circumstances of the people involved, but also upon the type of settlement. The ownership of flats was limited: one family was allowed one flat and one second home.

The regional and social consequences of the development of new housing estates

The first fifteen-year housing programme laid down that flats be built in housing estates. The first such estates were developed in the sixties on the border of the inner parts of the city in the so-called transitory residential zone, with the aim of improving the infrastructure of the industrial peripheries mostly inhabited by workers. But workers had in fact little chance of obtaining new flats.

As a result of the housing shortage, the authorities rewarded the social groups that were more important from its own point of view, and safeguarded the integration of certain social strata into the political authority through the state's flat allocation system. As during that period even a limited market economy in housing and private construction was not allowed, the younger members of the better paid and better placed strata in society naturally moved out from the old decaying inner zones towards the new parts of the city by means of the distribution system. Sociological research has shown that at an early stage the estates built during the first wave of development became the residences of the highly qualified leading and professional layers of the society, and of young families with several children. Thus, the process was accompanied by social segregation. However, because of their desire to present themselves as a power of the working class, the authorities refused to acknowledge the phenomenon. They kept up the ideological promises and normative image of an independent home for every family in the democratic new housing estates, built for the people.

However, the new parts of cities raised a growing number of problems. There was a lack of social publicity and market relations, but information was fed back (partly through the mass media and partly through research on urban and housing sociology) both to the authorities and, in many cases, to the interested parties. The first group of problems related to the conditions in the new developments: to the level of infrastructure, to the created milieu, but especially to the size of the flats. Criticism was voiced that the flats were too standardized and too small, and did not express either socially differentiated expectations or family sizes. Table 6.1 shows that the proportion of one-room flats was high in the capital compared to other towns. Another area of criticism was related to the allocation of flats. The disadvantages of the mainly working-class strata in the system of allocation were becoming increasingly obvious. Sociological surveys conducted in the new housing estates could hardly find any unskilled workers among the inhabitants (Szelényi–Konrád, 1969).

In 1970, with the situation becoming increasingly untenable, a system of flat construction and allocation was developed that paid greater

Table 6.1 The size of flats in housing estates by groups of cities and towns, 1980 (KSH, 1983)

Urban group	1 room	2 rooms	3 rooms	4 + rooms
Budapest	14.6	55.2	27.4	2.8
County towns	7.9	63.7	25.9	2.5
Other county headquarters	10.6	67.5	19.6	2.3
Other towns	10.7	68.8	18.5	2.0
Total No.	26.215	99.231	55.921	
Percentage	11.5	62.8	23.3	2.4

Source: *A lakótelepek főbb adatai* (Data on housing estates), Population Census, 1980, Vol. 35, Central Statistical Office, Budapest

attention to the interests of social policy. The rents were also changed, reducing the sharp difference in the maintenance of state- and privately-owned flats. After these reforms, about 70 per cent of rented flats and those co-operatively owned which the local council allocated, were occupied by manual workers (Hoffman, 1981, p. 47).

The reform of allocation policy had a major impact upon the social composition of the second ring of housing estates developed in the seventies, where poor families, the lower middle classes and semi-skilled workers have been over-represented, and the proportion of people of higher social status has been extremely low (KSH, 1983). These estates have suffered from various problems. Their rapid construction has meant that related public services have been delayed or not developed at all. The buildings have rapidly been damaged because they were occupied too quickly and because the new inhabitants have found it hard to adapt to their new environment. Social deviation, crime and alcoholism have been common, and the divorce rate has been high; hence, the living conditions of under-age children have been rather problematic.

Further differences arise from the connections and access to the inner parts of the city. The inhabitants of the inner housing estates can make more use of the opportunities of urban life because of their ecological and social situation, whereas those who live in the outer ring find it more difficult. Sociological research shows that inhabitants of housing estates vary according to their ability to compensate for local shortcomings. Those with higher social status, higher pay and a better education are more able to utilize the urban facilities of the inner city than people who have a lower social status, are poorer, less educated and less inclined as well. Hence, life is rather closed and localized in the second belt of housing estates.

The social status of the newer parts of the city has significantly deteriorated with the appearance of the controlled housing market and the growing social and political considerations of the system of allocation.

Table 6.2 The distribution of flats by type of ownership in different types of settlements in 1980 (per cent)

Settlement	Personal	Property State	Total
Budapest	42.3	57.7	100.0
Cities	69.5	30.5	100.0
Villages	92.2	7.8	100.0
Total	74.4	25.6	100.0

Source: Barta, B., Vukovich, Gy., 1983, p. 216.

The inner belt continues to enjoy greater prestige, particularly the prefabricated housing estate along the Danube built in the eighties, where the flats were sold as freehold. This housing estate owes its high value to its ecological situation, to the larger size of its flats and especially to its more favourable social composition.

It is sometimes said that the new housing estates represent a kind of suburbanizing process, with an exodus of the better-off social strata from the decaying inner parts of the city to the outer zone. This is true in the limited sense that the population of the first belt of housing estates came from the better skilled layers of the inner parts. However, they did not go to the new housing estates for ecological reasons, or because they were attracted by the environment or the flats. They went because the state socialist model of economic and housing policy either did not yet offer any market alternative, or even if it did, the alternative lay not in the choice of flat, but in the means of acquiring it.

Forms of private construction in Budapest

People did not necessarily enter the state-controlled housing market by choice. Many studies have shown the difficulties experienced by those who embarked upon building their own house or flat – the institutional barriers, the effects of exploitative building work that consumes both spare time and money – as well as the advantages.

Private construction spread in the capital in the seventies, though to a far smaller extent than elsewhere in the country (see Table 6.2) (Barta–Vukovich, 1983, p. 216). This has resulted in a number of types of housing, such as the building co-operative – bringing together the capital of several families for the purpose of building a house – and detached family houses built by the owner, the family and the neighbours. Family houses can be found mainly in the countryside. Co-operative houses are most common in towns and in Budapest, for sociological reasons, but also because of the interests of the state construction system (Dávid, 1983, pp. 150–75).

In the capital vacant plots, particularly plots supplied with public utilities, are extremely scarce, partly because of the urban and land policy of earlier periods, and partly because of the construction of the large housing estates. Existing and marketable plots are extremely expensive, and are therefore available only to those with massive amounts of ready cash. Some vacant plots are jealously guarded by the city planning authorities for building housing estates. This effectively ensures the intensive development of sites. There is a limited number of plots supplied with public utilities, the authorities preferring to issue permits for building co-operative houses, representing a more intensive form than the family house, which can also be controlled better. The policy on plots was also used as a particular means of rewarding the high-ranking cadres faithful to the regime. As state construction levels fell, some well-situated plots supplied with public utilities, or potentially cheap to supply, were acquired by the cadres at a price well below the market rate.

This policy was reinforced by the state's credit policy, which offered better terms for co-operative building than for family houses. This was particularly so in settlements where vacant plots were in great demand for housing estates, particularly in the larger towns and in the capital. Policy on plots and credit kept changing in line with political and ideological constellations and the interests of the time, with favour falling on industrial workers, miners, or young married couples accordingly. This was basically to mitigate the disadvantages of these building loans.

The conditions of private housing and the changes in policy relating to plots and credit were subordinated to the interests of state housing. But it is not easy to see why the state introduced the market and openings for private construction into housing. It may have realized that state construction was inadequate to meet housing needs or handle the related social conflicts. Or the state may simply have wanted to integrate and control the illegal housing market. Both factors may have been present. However, one point is certain: without a private housing market the state's flat construction programme would have been a marked failure.

Regional and social consequences

The higher income groups of society, with higher levels of skill and education, are to be found mainly in Buda, in the green, hilly parts. In part, this is because some of the wealthier and more qualified groups of society have moved to the green zones of Buda from the housing estates and built their homes there as private construction has expanded. People from the inner parts of the city who belong to wealthy social groups, political leaders, and even the new moneyed elites also feature in this category, either for reasons of prestige, or because of the environmental problems in the city. Building represents a capital investment for many of them.

Pest also has its prestigious districts, though they are fewer in number than in Buda. These areas lie in the Inner City, along the Danube, around the Parliament, in the Újlipótváros area, and in some better housing estates in the city made up of privately-owned flats.

Unskilled manual workers are rare on the Buda side, although they live in large numbers spread all over Pest. Lower-status parts of the city can be found mainly in the outlying districts, such as Angyalföld, Újpest, Pestimre, Pesterzsébet, Csepel, Rákospalota, Kőbánya and Budafok. Districts of lower social composition can also be found on the edge of the Inner City, in the run-down Józsefváros and Ferencváros, adjoining the Grand Boulevard.

Research by Gábor Csanádi and János Ladányi indicates that segregation has taken different forms in Budapest. It has been rapid among those of high status, both at the time of the Compromise and today, which is why large ecological models describe well their spatial segregation. However, in the case of the groups of lower social status, researchers have not been able to find 'extensive regions of homogeneous low status, similar to those of high status groups' either in the late 1880s, or today.

Many of Budapest's middle classes have, for several reasons, been stuck in flats in the new parts of the city that do not meet their needs, or in the decaying districts of the inner areas. Either they have missed out on the different forms of state housing allocation policy; or they have not been able to make use of market opportunities through the state's credit policy; or they were unable to purchase expensive plots, and there were no cheap ones available – at least plots supplied with public utilities and planning permission. Hence they have stayed in the inner districts against their wishes, as they could not accept the composition of the local society or the ecological conditions. The policy of the authorities on plots did not allow these middle classes to move out to the outer districts to family houses, or to build modern flats utilizing the land more rationally than it is used today.

An increasing number of old and retired people live in the decaying inner districts, at the mercy of state rehabilitation. In 1985 an experimental rehabilitation programme was launched in the Seventh District, in Erzsébetváros, where the local authorities renovated some blocks of flats. The old inhabitants could not afford the increased rents or the cost of reconstruction; therefore, they mostly accepted the usually lower-quality flats offered to them in an alien ecological environment. The huge market value of the renovated state-owned flats could be paid only by highly qualified high-income groups coming from other parts of the city. Hence, a new social structure in the renovated blocks has developed (Cséfalvay–Pomázi, 1990, pp. 27–39).

This 'gentrification' of the Inner City cannot be considered a general phenomenon: only a small section of the highly qualified middle-class strata had these opportunities. Restoration has been going on in isolated cases because of a lack of public and private capital. A significant change can only be expected if a moneyed middle class develops which is attracted to the environment of the inner city, and a local authority with capital appears. However, highly-qualified social groups cannot be expected to make efforts to move into the inner areas because of the grave environmental problems there, nor can the present residents be expected to give up their desire to move to the cleaner air of the outer parts.

The segregation experienced in Budapest is not acute. A moralistic view could even interpret the situation as good. However, the authors of the present volume are less positive about it. Mild segregation is not the result of human choice, of the democratic, tolerant atmosphere of a society, but of social and political pressures and interests. Ecological models do not express the inner stratification of society, the real social differences, or the financial demands of the population. A large number of people live in flats, the market value of which is far above their incomes. Nor do they express the differentiated system of social expectations: only a very small fraction of the society lives in homes that meet their needs and social position. Hence, the spatial social conditions are unintelligible and cannot be handled by means of urban policy.

The basic key to the phenomenon of segregation, over and above the historical and planning factors that have been mentioned, is the housing economy system under state socialism. The location of social strata has been determined partly by the choice of districts for state housing programmes, and partly by the selective allocation policy. The segregating effects of quasi-market housing are also the results of this period. The state structures have regulated who could buy plots of land where, and what they could build.

The relationship of the state to the housing market has a long past in almost every country. Housing shortages after World War II resulted in a state housing economy of some kind in several market economies. This produced legal and administrative intervention, and the construction of flats by the authorities until the various dysfunctions became apparent: that, for instance, low rents limited private enterprise, and that demand for flats increased. While state intervention was not completely eliminated subsequently, more indirect means of stimulating the market have been adopted in order to try to reduce the social inequalities caused by the market economy in housing.

The Hungarian example shows that the same dilemma is present, although it takes a form different to that of market economies: here the adverse consequences of housing managed by the state are to be improved by the mechanisms of the market. In Hungary, the building and allocation of flats by the state socialist authorities was just as unable to handle the problems of housing effectively, eliminate shortages or consistently take into consideration social policy issues. The existing market offered some compensation, and a significant part of those social groups omitted from state allocation could solve, or at least mitigate, their housing problems with some sacrifices. However, they were only able to partially correct the limitations set by the authorities, because of the excessive presence of the state and of the 'quasi' nature of the market. The housing shortage was not ended, and no spatial social structure related to market demand, as well as to the ecological demands of the different social groups, was able to develop.

The entire system of the housing economy is being transformed today. A number of transitional elements have been decided upon, but several questions have not yet been clarified. There is no doubt that the market economy in housing will grow. Privatization has also been launched, although it is not yet known who will receive the bulk of state-owned flats: the local governments, private individuals, or perhaps both. But the restricted housing economy will definitely go, and rents will rocket. Presumably the changes in rents and in ownership relations will result in the transformation of the spatial social structure and in the growth of segregation. All this presupposes better protection of the interests of those who live in the physically decayed parts of the city in low-quality, neglected flats, who were left out of the allocation system of state socialism simply because they were uninformed, poor and/or modest in their needs and for these reasons had not applied for a new flat. For them, the market alternative of solving their housing problem does not even arise. They are the most threatened people in a housing economy structured along a strong market model.

Part Three

Functional spaces

7
Urban functions and functional zones

The formation of functional zones

The definition and study of urban functions is the main focus of every
text on urban geography. Functional morphology, which tries to link
urban landscape to the functions of the city, was particularly favoured
by Hungarian settlement geography in the first part of the twentieth
century. This was the traditional interpretation of human geography
which considered settlements as man-made developments of the landscape. Over recent decades, settlements have been studied as spatial
social organizations, the functions of which express different series of
social actions.

Urban functions can be defined in a number of ways: they can be
expressed by the number of persons they employ (such as industry,
transport, public health); by the number of institutions that exercise
them, or by their sphere of influence. Functions can be distinguished that
serve the inhabitants of the city, covering the immediate sphere of attraction, or that stretch beyond the environs of the city. Our assessment is
a socio-geographic one: it examines the performance of the different
functions as social processes, rooted in individual decisions. These
individual decisions are grouped together (for instance, the same place of
work is chosen by hundreds or even thousands), and may constitute a
contiguous social group of identical interests (for example, the
community of employees), or may perform identical functions without
having an internal organization (for instance, the visitors to an exhibition). Single decisions of this sort influence a series of urban functions

and are linked to concrete space in each case. The place of work is at a definite point of the city, to which the simple journey from home touches upon at least three functional spaces (place of work, residence and line of transport).

The functions of a modern metropolitan city are the same everywhere, and there are rational individual decisions behind the spatial location of these functions: the rational decisions of those who perform the functions and those who use them. The decisions are influenced by two kinds of mechanisms which mediate the rationality of the utilization of space: the market, and planning.

The market and planning operate in every big city, although their proportions may differ. There is no liberal economy that can do without planning in the operation of the complicated organization of a metropolis; and there is no state socialist command economy that is so strict that it can exclude individual decisions and the operation – even if illegal – of the market from the processes of urbanization.

The rationality of the use of space cannot be described in general; it depends on the user and it has to suit his or her demands, mostly mediated by the price of property in a market economy. But planning also interferes: for instance, it grants space in the centre to offices which are visited by many people, and it does not allow business premises (company offices) to push the functions of public services to the periphery of the city. It is again planning which looks after the communication network of the city, and safeguards communication between the various functional spaces.

In state socialism, urban space is publicly owned (perhaps with the exception of family houses), and the value judgement of the market is substituted for by planners' decisions. These are usually professional decisions aimed at safeguarding rationality in the utilization of space. (Distortions produced by political interference are not necessarily greater than those generated by speculation with property.) However, the starting point of rationality is not the interest of the individual user, but that of the state institution (housing estate, state department store, hospital, etc.). The two often coincide, but this is not guaranteed. Therefore, there is often a lack of correspondence between functional spaces in command economies. Users are obliged to use the space earmarked by the state: they cannot choose the home best suited to the family, or a school for their children, or even their own doctor. We described in the previous chapter how individuals – whenever they had a chance – tried to express their interests, and offset the rigidity of planning in the manner of the market.

To sum up: the sphere and spatial system of urban functions has developed similarly in both western and state-socialist cities, although the locational values of some spaces have been mediated by different mechanisms.

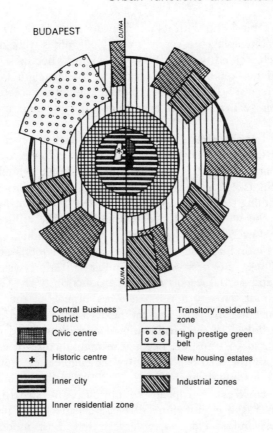

Figure 7.1 Model of urban structure of Budapest

Economic functions

The industrial city

Industry had a primary role in the development of Budapest into a big city, and this leading role lasted for a surprisingly long time, right up to the end of the 1960s. Though the number of those employed in industry has fallen by 50 per cent during the past two decades, the extension of the tertiary sector is mostly related to functional changes in local industry (the development of marketing and the R&D sectors, and the concentration of the management of enterprises in Budapest).

In 1870, 45,000 people were employed in industry (including handicrafts) in Budapest. There were only a few major factories, such as the shipyard at Óbuda and the Ganz ironworks. Subsequently, the manufacturing industry developed rapidly and Budapest, on account of its position as capital and with its excellent location in terms of communications geography, played a central role. Coal mines were opened near the capital which yielded fuel for the steam engines. Budapest was the prominent capital market of the country, and foreign capital appeared there and nowhere else. The rapidly-growing population created a significant local market, which in turn encouraged the manufacture of consumer goods.

At the end of the nineteenth century, the market for industry extended over the entire Austro-Hungarian monarchy, and even over parts of the Balkans, particularly in branches which supplemented the stronger Austrian and Czech industries. The first branch of large-scale industry was the milling industry, and one of the largest centres of milling industry in the world developed in Budapest. The milling industry was followed by several other branches of the food industry, such as meat processing (with huge slaughterhouses and feed lots), and the canning industry. Thus, the first wave of industrialization was based on the processing and partial export of food production of the Great Plain. The local market of the city developed every branch of the food industry.

The engineering industry was the next to appear, and its development was closely linked to the production of agricultural and food-processing machinery, and to transport needs (the manufacture of engines, wagons and boats). By the turn of the century the engineering industry had taken over as the leading branch (with 37,000 employees in 1910), and it resembled its West European counterparts in structure as well as technical level (the manufacture of electrical machines, internal combustion engines, bulbs, etc.). The largest and most modern engineering works were the ordnance factories (especially the Weiss Manfred Works of Csepel) in the early twentieth century. The chemical industry (fertilizer and pharmaceuticals) also appeared at the end of the nineteenth century.

Wood, transported from the Carpathians partly along waterways and partly by rail, was processed in large quantities in the capital, and furniture factories appeared, employing thousands of craftsmen. The belated industrialization of Budapest ensured that some traditional industries (for example, the textile industry) could not develop because of Austrian and Czech competition, but the most modern branches of industry of the period appeared at an early date. Manufacturing industry was mostly export-oriented, whereas small-scale industry served the local market. The number of people employed by the latter grew constantly: from 33,000 to 88,000 between 1890 and 1910. From 1887, however, the greater share of industrial employment was found in large-scale industry, although that proportion grew only slowly.

The belated emergence of the manufacturing industry and the importance of foreign capital meant that capital concentration was significant. In 1900, one-third of workers were employed in factories with more than

500 employees. The industries of Budapest enjoyed many advantages from their late development: modern technology, up-to-date industrial structure, export orientation and the concentration of capital. However, Hungarian-owned medium-sized industries remained underdeveloped. Consequently, the national middle class was also weak.

The state promoted the development of industry. Policies applied to the entire country, but it was the industries of Budapest that benefited most. In 1881 new industrial enterprises established in the modern branches of manufacturing industry were exempted from taxation until 1895, and this exemption was extended by another fifteen years in 1890. In addition, industrial products transported to and from Budapest by rail enjoyed preferential tariffs.

Industry was located primarily on the Pest side of the city. The Danube (as a line of transport and source of water) and the railway stations where raw materials arrived were powerful attractions for industrial developments in their neighbourhood. Small-scale industry such as printing and clothing factories was established in the inner residential zone.

The industry of Budapest – with the exception of some transitory booms – was in constant crisis during the inter-war period. The disintegration of the united market of Austria–Hungary could not be offset by export-oriented industries. In 1922, manufacturing industry production was barely half its 1913 value. Despite the boom between 1925 and 1929 (the industrial production value of 1929 was 12 per cent higher than that of 1913), stagnation continued in the typical industrial branches of Budapest, such as engineering and the food industry. The boom was due to the expansion of the textile industry using the cheap labour of the crowded capital. New textile mills were equipped with machinery that was dismantled in England and France. Thus the modernity of the industrial structure deteriorated, and instead of technological advancement, cheap labour was the driving force of industrialization in Budapest.

The Great Depression shook the very foundations of industry in Budapest. Production value dropped by half (to one-third in the case of engineering industry) between 1929 and 1932. The slow emergence from the depression accelerated only towards the end of the thirties, mainly due to ordnance production and to preparations for war.

The capacity of engineering industry remained only partly utilized during this period. Only some big engineering works – like Ganz – succeeded in improving their external market position with their up-to-date products (diesel engines, electric locomotives, high-capacity transformers). Within the engineering industry structural changes were favourable: the manufacture of electrical machinery and of communications equipment developed fast, mainly because of foreign capital investment (Phillips, AEG, Siemens).

Small-scale industries remained significant during the inter-war period, employing 115,000 people (owners and employees together) in 1938, almost 40 per cent of total industrial employment. The main change in the geographical location of industry was due to the fact that the rapidly expanding textile and paper industries and new branches of the engineering industry settled in the inner zone of the agglomeration of the day, which today are the outer districts of the city.

After World War II the history of the capital's industrial growth can be divided in two. The first phase lasted until the late 1960s and was characterized by a significant growth in the labour force. At that time Budapest was over-industrialized: 55 per cent of the active population of the capital was engaged in industry and construction in 1970. During the last twenty years the number of workers has been reduced almost by half and industry had taken on a different role. But the shrinking of industry has not reduced its major position overall.

The past forty-five years have been dominated by state ownership of the overwhelming part of industry (nationalization took place between 1946 and 1949). In the early 1950s, the majority of small-scale industries were eliminated and artisans were forced to join craftsmen's co-operatives. Private small-scale industry was soon permitted again, but was prevented from gaining strength by numerous restrictions, even during the eighties when private enterprise was gaining momentum. In 1987, enterprises located in Budapest employed 346,000 people in the city (22.7 per cent of the industrial employees of the country) – approximately the same as in 1938. 235,000 people were also employed in the industrial plants of Budapest enterprises located in the country. Of the total number, 282,000 were employed by state-owned firms, 45,000 by co-operative industries, and only 19,000 by private small-scale industry. Unfortunately no data are available on private enterprise set up since 1989, but the privatization of state industry is only just beginning.

The structure of industry has not changed significantly (see Table 7.1). Though the food and textile industries have shrunk (the milling industry has practically disappeared), and the engineering industry has strengthened its role, essentially all the manufacturing branches succeeded in wrenching some investments and development from the government. Consequently, industrial investment in Budapest primarily enlarged and modernized the existing factories, conserving the old industrial structure. There is little high technology, as subsidies have gone towards the maintenance of outdated industrial plants rather than the development of new branches. The old branches of industry formed strong lobbies and often close personal ties with the party authorities. The leaders of the large enterprises and top members of the party apparatus often changed places.

The fall in the number of industrial employees was not the result of

Table 7.1 Changes in the industrial structure of Budapest (per cent of employees)

Branch of industry	1955	1969	1987
Extracting	0.3	0.7	1.4
Energy production	1.8	1.6	3.9
Metallurgy	5.4	4.3	4.5
Building materials	3.0	2.8	2.3
Chemicals	5.8	7.5	10.8
Engineering	8.9	9.5	8.9
Means of transport	11.5	9.7	9.2
Electrical engines	5.1	5.7	5.4
Telecommunications technology	5.1	8.3	11.3
Precision machines	4.1	5.6	7.1
Mass produced metal goods	6.4	5.3	4.0
Wood	3.4	3.0	2.0
Paper	1.2	1.5	1.5
Printing	1.9	2.1	3.1
Textiles	13.0	10.3	8.2
Leather	3.8	3.5	1.4
Clothing	4.9	3.6	1.5
Food	7.2	6.4	9.1
Other	1.6	3.2	3.6
Handicrafts	5.6	5.4	0.8
Total	100.0	100.0	100.0

Source: *Statistical Yearbook of Budapest 1988*, Central Statistical Office, Budapest.

any technological modernization of industry. Some new equipment was undoubtedly put into operation, but it was rarely up-to-date. One important reason for this fall was the decline of in-migration from the countryside. The utilization of machinery in the city is low, and part of the equipment installed is not used at all. In the 1970s the enterprises of Budapest moved some of their (often obsolete) machinery to new plants set up in the country. The larger enterprises increased production through an expansion of the workforce, rather than through technological development. This simpler solution better suited their interests, and saved capital investment. Productive labour left Budapest, whereas enterprise management and the white-collar occupations stayed. For instance, the number of manual workers fell by 23 per cent, but that of white-collar occupations by only 10 per cent between 1975 and 1987 (while gross industrial production grew by 2.2 per cent). In 1975, there were 2.31 manual workers for every white-collar employee, whereas this figure was only 1.19 in 1987. This was partly the logical consequence of the growing role of entrepreneurial managers and of R&D, but also shows the enormous bureaucracy of the state industrial enterprises. The management of a large company was more interested in the maintenance of the central apparatus (of which they were a part), than in the extension of business activities. Therefore the decline of Budapest's industries is not merely the normal process characteristic of big cities; it is also part of a general economic stagnation and growing bureaucratization. Capital and labour have not been transferred into modern and efficient branches of the economy.

The geographical location of industry has been influenced by various factors. Natural conditions played a role: for instance, the abundant water of the River Danube favoured the development of industries requiring water; the abundance of building materials and the flat land of Pest allowed for industrial estates requiring a lot of space, for the airport, and for the goods yards of the railways. Communications also played a role: there was navigation along the Danube, and railways from every corner of the country all met in Budapest. These were especially important in the initial phase of industrialization.

Factors of importance today are the expansion of residential areas to the detriment of the old industrial regions; the assertion of the considerations of urban settlement, and environmental protection. Building regulations have tried to push industrial developments towards the periphery. The 1886 building regulation controlled the areas that could be allocated for the 'unhealthy and odorous factories'. The building regulation of 1894 divided the capital into four zones, and permitted industries only in the fourth. The building regulation of 1914 established eight zones in Budapest, of which one – the seventh (Kőbánya, Ferencváros, Kispest, Pesterzsébet, i.e. the south and south-eastern parts of Pest) – was specifically earmarked for industry. The 1988 Master Plan pushes the industrial zones further towards the periphery. However, no new industrial region has been developed in Budapest during recent decades. Some of the old industrial regions have been demolished and often housing estates have been built in their place. But the reconstruction of industry has strengthened the industrial zones which had developed during the course of the twentieth century (occupying about 1600 ha.). They are located at the edge of the administrative boundary of Budapest as it was at the turn of the century. When the inner suburban belt was added to this territory in 1950, the industrial zones became parts of the inner zone of the city. Thus, the six industrial zones which can be identified at present are located between the residential zone of the old city centre and the new one built during the past fifty years, relatively near the city centre.

The six industrial zones have gradually expanded along three important axes of transport since the middle of the nineteenth century. They are the following:

- the territory between the Danube and the oldest railway line, running north between Budapest and Vác;

- the territory along the Budapest–Cegléd and Budapest–Hatvan railway lines to the east and south-east;
- the territory between the Budapest–Kelebia–Belgrade railway line and the Danube to the south.

All three axes are on the Pest side. During the past 100 years, industry had drawn further away from the city centre along these axes, but the suburbs out along the axes were also strongly industrialized. The residential nature of the areas between and beyond these axes has been retained in the suburbs.

On the right side of the river, the Buda Hills hindered the development of industrial zones, and the aristocratic and *grand bourgeois* population of Buda blocked its growth too. To the north (Óbuda) and south, two minor industrial concentrations developed on the Danube. The industrial estates of Óbuda produced building materials (from the local raw materials), and attracted industries which required a plentiful water supply (such as textile dyeing). The southern zone was located on the river but was quite independent of it, and its growth was mainly due to the large area of flat land and the Kelenföld railway station. The six industrial zones show a certain specialization of industry. It is worth mentioning that about two-fifths of the industrial estates are located within 1 kilometre of the Danube. The six industrial zones are as follows.

(1) In the zone of north Pest several branches of industry are present. The large majority of the factories are located along a single road, Váci Road, heading north from the Western railway station. The most important engineering factories are the Ganz Shipyard and Crane Factory, the Láng Engineering Works and Tungsram (electric machines, lighting equipment). The whole range of the leather and shoe industry is to be found on Váci Road, and many people are employed by car and railway repair workshops. One-fifth of the capital's industrial workers are employed in this zone. The territory of Angyalföld (District Thirteen) is an old industrial zone, with a number of crowded industrial estates, but industry is being gradually squeezed out and its place being taken by residential areas. Of the twenty-two districts of the capital, the largest number of industrial workers are employed here. In Újpest (the Fourth District) industry is still strong, employing 70 per cent of the population of the district. Besides Váci Road there is another important industrial locality here, along the Budapest–Vác railway line, where the most important factory is Chinoin Pharmaceuticals and the locomotive and wagon repair workshop of the railways. Only two decades ago, Újpest had the image of a country township. Now the dominant feature of the district is the disheartening monotony of large housing estates.

Váci Road is a real early-twentieth-century industrial zone. The factory

Functional spaces

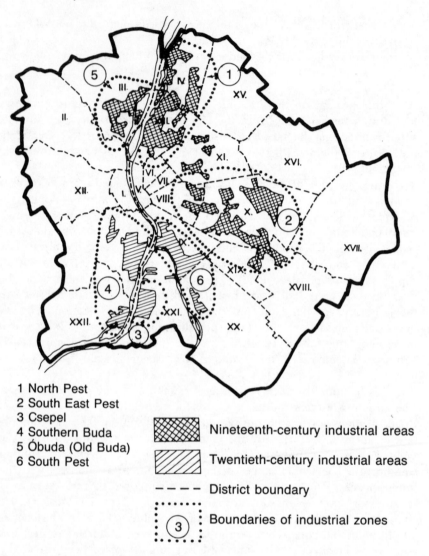

Figure 7.2 Industrial zones of Budapest

1 North Pest
2 South East Pest
3 Csepel
4 Southern Buda
5 Óbuda (Old Buda)
6 South Pest

Nineteenth-century industrial areas

Twentieth-century industrial areas

– – – – District boundary

Boundaries of industrial zones

buildings were built in the style of the last century, with additional buildings forced into the spacious courtyards of the factories as if dropped there by chance. Three- or four-storeyed blocks of flats are wedged in, built in the same style as the factories, with corridors all around the courtyards. Old working-class dynasties live here, which have been working for generations in the shipyard, at Hungarian Steel, and at Láng Engineering Works (turbines, machinery for power stations). Pubs, small grocers and working-class meeting places are everywhere.

(2) The industrial zone of south-east Pest is the largest in the capital (employing a quarter of the industrial workforce). It consists of two parts: one is Kőbánya near the railway lines, and the other is Ferencváros on the Danube, of which Kőbánya is the older industrial region. Brick production and the quarrying of limestone was begun in the early nineteenth century, and the excellent water of the local karst springs laid the foundations of breweries. The Budapest–Cegléd railway line (opened in 1848) transported large quantities of food from the Great Plain to the capital, so that a multi-faceted food industry developed around the cargo depots of Kőbánya. Large pig farms were located in the region right up to the 1930s. Other industries are also represented here: the large engineering factories (Ganz MÁVAG, Orion), the two largest Hungarian pharmaceutical companies, and the textile industry. The food industry (with large slaughterhouses and canning factories) is the leading branch of the Ferencváros zone, since the earlier mills have been closed down. The chemical industry and engineering also have a prominent role.

(3) The industrial zone of Csepel used to be totally dominated by heavy industry (with the exception of a vegetable oil press and a wood and paper factory). The Weiss Manfred Works, founded in 1884, was one of the largest ordnance factories of the Austro-Hungarian monarchy, and later it grew into a huge engineering complex. Located at the northern part of Csepel Island, this mammoth factory employed 30,000 workers in 1970 and was the largest industrial plant in Hungary. Today the company-town that formed around the factory (the Twenty-First District) has more than 50,000 inhabitants. The factory has suffered severely from the structural transformation of heavy industry, and a number of units have been closed down. Today, hardly more than 9,000 people are employed by all the factories of the district. Ten or fifteen years ago people commuted by train from the inner housing estates to Csepel; today, crowds of commuters start out from Csepel for other districts. With the forthcoming opening of the Danube–Main–Rhine channel, the growing traffic of the free port may help revive the industries of Csepel.

(4) The industrial zone of southern Buda is the youngest of all. It was built around the cargo depot of Kelenföld in the 1930s. The factories were built along two parallel roads, Budafoki and Fehérvári Roads. The structure of industry is up-to-date: the engineering industry has a prominent role, and the electronics industry is quite significant. The southern part of the zone (Budafok) has a more traditional industrial structure (wood-processing and wine cellars having the largest export trade). Both the modern and the older zones are surrounded by residential zones.

(5) The zone of Óbuda to the north on the right bank of the Danube has shrunk (4 per cent of the industrial workforce work here). It is a very traditional industrial zone made up of the textile industry and shipbuilding.

This zone will probably disappear soon from the industrial map of Budapest.

(6) The industrial zone of southern Pest stretches along the eastern bank of the Ráckeve branch of the Danube, opposite the island of Csepel. Here the dominant branch of industry is food processing, based on the raw materials arriving from the Plain. This is the continuation of the Ferencváros zone (even though geographically it is not contiguous). Chemical industries, including fertilizer production, are new branches in this small zone.

These six industrial zones evolved a long time ago. The rapid expansion of industry in the 1950s and 1960s took place essentially within existing companies. The industrial zones mostly extend along roads. Along the main roads leading to the city from the Plains the food industry is still significant – it is interesting that links with the macro-regions are still influential in the inner industrial geography of the city.

As we have seen, the old industrial zones are pulling back and residential areas are occupying their place. This is partly because the inner residential zone can only spread towards the industrial zones (mainly on the Pest side). Moreover, the infrastructure of the industrial belt is quite well established, which makes the massive building of flats in place of the demolished industrial estates cheaper.

A number of industrial estates can also be found outside the industrial zones, scattered all over the city. The majority of artisans and repair shops can be found in the inner districts, where we also find some big printing presses and the centre of the fashion industry. Several large industrial plants have been wedged into the inner residential belt, such as the Ganz Electrical Works (electrical machines, electric locomotives), the Gamma (instruments) and the Ikarus bus factory.

A further rapid decline in industrial production functions can be expected in Budapest. The opening up of the property market will squeeze out old industria[l] plants from the inner parts of the city; presumably it will be more efficient than the building authorities, who were often forced to retreat in the face of pressure from state-owned industrial enterprises, although it is not yet known what new pressure groups will appear on the scene. Structural change may be speeded up, and further jobs may be cut in the textile and food industries. The threat of significant unemployment is small, as the service sector will expand in the market economy, creating many new jobs. However, industrial management will continue to be concentrated in the capital, even if some branches in the country break away from their mother institutions in Budapest. Foreign capital is mostly interested in Budapest; 80 per cent of all joint ventures are located in the capital. But the age of the industrial city – albeit with considerable delay – has come to an end in the Hungarian capital.

Transport

Public transport is well organized and handles a high volume of traffic relatively quickly and cheaply. The road network, however, is insufficient, and can only carry car traffic with great difficulty.

Public transport has a long tradition: a regular omnibus service was launched in Pest in 1832. The cogwheel railway up to the Széchenyi Hill started in 1874 with a steam engine in those days, and the first electric trams appeared in 1889 (by then the horse-drawn tram service had a 48 km. network). In 1890, the capital's public transport carried 70 million passengers, and in 1920, 365 million. In the first part of the century, boats over the Danube also played an important role in public transport. Buses started to operate in the capital in 1915.

The first suburban railway lines were opened at the end of the last century. As fifteen main railway lines started from the capital, a significant railway network was built (almost 200 km. long) within the capital itself. Railway traffic was handled by twenty-eight stations. The tram network was practically complete by the early twentieth century, and over the past thirty years the bus network has expanded considerably. Buses go out to some of the suburbs, and they also form the main connection with the outer districts. Every part of the city is linked into the transport network, and many of the surface lines are linked to the metro.

By the early twentieth century, the backbone of the urban road network was completed. It consisted of boulevards connected by a system of parallel avenues. The avenues continued into highways going out of the capital in different directions. Thus, the road network brought country traffic directly into the city centre, and to the four bridges there. However expedient it may have been at the turn of the century, today it is the source of almost constant traffic jams and air pollution in the inner city.

Private cars were still a rare phenomenon in the early twentieth century. When the Royal Hungarian Automobile Club was founded in 1900, only 213 cars were registered in the city. Car ownership was held back later by the slow economic development of the inter-war period, and by the collectivism of the socialist system after World War II (and by its poverty). In 1970, only 70,000 cars were privately owned in a capital of almost 2 million inhabitants (by 1990 this figure had reached 500,000).

The bridges of Budapest are important transport links. The first permanent bridge was opened only in 1849 (the Chain Bridge). Before that time only a boat bridge linked Buda and Pest which had to be removed for the winter. The Chain Bridge was followed by Margit Bridge in 1876, by Franz Joseph Bridge (today's Szabadság Bridge) in

1896, and by Erzsébet Bridge in 1903. At the end of the nineteenth century, the southern (1877) and the northern (1896) railway bridges were built. Since the early twentieth century, the capital has been enriched by only two additional bridges: the Petőfi Bridge (1937) and the Árpád Bridge, the construction of which was interrupted by the war and completed only in 1950. In the winter of 1944/5, the retreating German troops blew up all the bridges over the Danube.

At present, public transport in Budapest carries annually 2,000 million passengers. Buses carry the largest number (872 million), but their share is decreasing as they have become the slowest means of public transport. Since 1985 the role of trams has once again been increasing (600 million passengers), and the underground also carries significant traffic (350 million people). The number of passengers using the suburban trains is also over 100 million. The first underground line was opened in 1896, but the second line was not built until 1970. The expansion of the network has been slow; at present, there is only 35 km. of track, serving limited parts of the city.

Urban traffic is heavily burdened by the limited housing market, the building of new flats in large housing estates and by the housing shortage. In the past decades most new flats were found in the new housing estates, so that there was little chance of finding a flat near one's job. Another problem is the fact that the white-collar employees of the government and business districts of Pest mostly live on the Buda side. Therefore, the bridges are always incredibly crowded. The situation could be alleviated by a tunnel under the Danube, but this has not yet been articulated even in the form of a plan.

The Budapest Transport Company runs four suburban trains. One goes to Szentendre, north of Buda (15 km.), the second goes to Ráckeve (on Csepel Island, 40 km.), the third goes east to Gödöllő (26 km.), and the fourth line runs within the city, going to the Twenty-First District (the village of Csepel before 1950). The majority of daily commuters travel to Budapest on the national railway lines. The three most important railway stations (the Western and Eastern on the Pest side, and the Southern on the Buda side) serve international, national and suburban traffic. These railway stations are located near the city centre, and are linked by metro lines.

Significant to the transport functions and functional spaces of Budapest is the capital's role in national and international traffic. The city is a transport juncture of major significance in the country. All of Hungary's main railway lines and roads start from Budapest. Passenger traffic is served by twenty-one railway stations besides the above-mentioned three main stations. The geographical location of Budapest means that railway and road transit traffic is very great, mainly between Central Europe, the Balkans and the Middle East. The first segment of the motorway encircling the city, which will divert the heavy lorries that at present pass through the city, will be opened in the near future.

Today the significance of navigation is modest, although it may grow again with the opening of the Danube–Main–Rhine channel. The free port of Csepel was developed between 1928 and 1938, and to the north there is a port (and a shipyard) on the Újpest stretch of the Danube. Air traffic began in 1923, with the Vienna–Budapest service from the former military airfield of Mátyásföld. The Budaörs airfield was opened in 1936, only 8.5 km. from the city centre. In those days the Hungarian airlines (MALERT) flew to eight European cities, but foreign airlines also had regular services. This airfield was soon outgrown by the traffic (today it is a sports airfield). The building of the present airport of Ferihegy (in the south-eastern area of the city) began during the war years, and was completed in 1947. The airport has since been significantly expanded and has an annual turnover of 1.5 million passengers.

Tourism

Tourism is an increasingly important economic function of the city. Budapest is a major tourist centre in Hungary and its turnover enjoys rapid growth. The city has numerous attractions. Its geographical location is advantageous: the Danube is an important element of the landscape in the city, and the Buda side with its hills offers lovely scenery. The sights of Budapest are a big attraction, particularly the Castle area – the medieval town – and the late-nineteenth-century art nouveau (Jugendstil) architecture of Pest. The urban life of Budapest is dynamic; it is, after all, the largest city in the whole of East Central Europe, and the only really international metropolis. Its musical life, museums and scientific centres constitute its cultural attraction. A number of international scientific congresses are regularly held in the city. The medicinal spas of Budapest also attract a number of visitors. And finally, business life further promotes tourism. Budapest is an important bridgehead of foreign capital not only into Hungary, but into all of Eastern Europe (the only stock exchange of the region is located here). It is to be hoped that the Hungarian capital will play a prominent role in the process of the integration of Eastern and Western Europe.

Tourism was insignificant under the Austro-Hungarian monarchy; Vienna was the main attraction. In 1885 there were 102,000 guests in the hotels of Budapest, of whom 35,000 were foreigners, and in 1913 these figures were 244,000 and 55,000 respectively. In the 1930s, events such as the regular international fairs and the 1933 Congress of the Eucharist all promoted tourism in the capital. 1937 was the peak year, with 183,000 foreign guests. It was followed by a long interval: the war and the devastation it brought, and the isolation of the cold war. The pre-war peak was surpassed only in 1962 (with 190,000 foreign visitors). Since then growth has been continuous, and it picked up sharply in the 1980s. In 1987 1.6 million foreign guests stayed in the hotels and the widespread bed and breakfast establishments. In that year there were 18,600 beds in forty-eight hotels, and 27,500 beds in private homes. Foreigners spent an average of 2.8 days in hotels and 8.9 days in private accommodation. 25 per cent of the hotel guests and 57 per cent of those in private accommodation came from socialist countries.

In 1987, there were only a few private hotels and guesthouses, and their size was limited (totalling only 1,300 places). During the past three years new hotels have been built in the city, mainly with foreign capital, and private hotels have also become more numerous. The relatively cheap family hotels are still scarce, because it is a big investment with slow returns. A considerable number of foreigners coming to Hungary visit their relatives – one-third of Hungarians live abroad – and they usually stay with their families. Hence, they are not recorded by statistics on tourism.

Though Budapest's supply of hotels and the infrastructure of tourism is by far the best in East Central Europe, it is still not sufficient. Rapidly-expanding tourism will require many more facilities. Most of the visitors come from nearby countries, mainly Germany and Austria. Hitherto the number of Czechoslovakian and Romanian visitors has been limited by various restrictions on travel. In 1990 Hungary agreed upon the abolition of visas with practically all the European countries, which has increased the number of visitors massively.

The tertiary city

Budapest has been developing from an industrial city into a tertiary-economy city since the late 1960s, and this process has gathered pace since the 1980s. Half of those who are recorded as having industrial occupations work in the headquarters of enterprises, and in industrial services. The post-industrial period has come to Budapest first. The capital has got rid of its less effective functions and has acquired a significance in tertiary functions far surpassing the one it had in the economic sphere.

Governmental and economic functions were largely intermingled under state socialism. Though the system of the command economy was ended in 1968, a significant number of large industrial enterprises continued to be located in the capital, around the Ministry of Industry. Nationwide services – such as transport, communications, and electricity – were handled by monopolies based in Budapest. The headquarters of the state wholesale trade, all the foreign trading companies, and all the banks were here, as were all the publishing houses, trade unions and cultural associations. The already prominent, unique metropolitan role of Budapest was vastly enhanced by the power concentration of state socialism. Centralized management did not merely extend to politics and the economy, but to every detail of social life. After the Communist takeover, the organizations of local society, the autonomous professional bodies and the spontaneous organizations of the society in general were eliminated, for fear that they might become foci of resistance. Any kind of activity – from collecting stamps to gliding – could be done only within nationally organized associations under political control, and all these organizations had their headquarters in Budapest.

Thus the functions of government – the natural corollaries of a capital – can be interpreted in a rather broad sense in Budapest. The governing functions, including the Parliament, ministries, and party headquarters, are – with few exceptions – to be found in the Fifth District in Pest, between the Margit and the Chain Bridges. Before World War II the majority of the ministries were located in Buda, near the Royal Castle. It was expediency that forced the ministries to the proximity of Parliament – when the ministries were destroyed in the siege of Buda at the end of the war, they moved into buildings that had previously been used for different purposes – but this transfer also symbolized a shift from a kingdom to a republic. (Hungary became a republic in 1946.) The commanding posts of government were moved from aristocratic Buda to bourgeois Pest (there are only two ministries on the Buda side). The Hungarian National Bank and the headquarters of several other banks are in the governmental quarter of the city, together with a number of foreign trading companies, the Hungarian Academy of Sciences, a number of publishing houses, and so forth. Thus the inner city is characterized by the territorial linkage of the Central Business District and government offices.

The functions of higher education and scientific research are of great significance. Half of the university students of the country study in Budapest. In 1988 there were 47,000 students in twenty-six institutions of higher education in the capital. The Hungarian universities are relatively small, and a number of university faculties have become independent universities. The largest is the Technical University of Budapest (7,800 students), followed by the Eötvös Loránd University of Sciences (6,700 students), and the Budapest University of Economics (4,000 students). The Semmelweis University of Medicine is another of the larger universities (3,300 students). There are other specialized institutions of higher education granting university diplomas (universities of veterinary sciences and horticulture, and the college of film and theatrical arts), and a number of teachers' training colleges and technical colleges.

Functional spaces

All the universities and colleges are scattered around the inner part of the city, mainly on the Pest side. Thus, there is no unified university campus in Budapest. The Technical University has developed a separate urban campus on the Buda side of the Danube between the Petőfi and the Szabadság Bridges, and on the Pest bank there is the University of Economics. The Eötvös Loránd University of Sciences is in the worst position, as only its Faculty of Law is housed in a single building. The Faculty of Science and particularly the Faculty of Arts are located at different points of the city, often far away from one another. The Faculty of Science has begun the construction of an urban campus on the Buda side, near the Technical University. During the course of its expansion, the Eötvös University has rented or purchased buildings which were not built for the purposes of a university. The reconstruction of the old buildings was very expensive and failed to make them any more comfortable. The lack of a compact university site is inconvenient in terms of the travel required between the different parts of the university, but also deprives the individual components of a university atmosphere. The majority of university buildings are located between the Danube and the Grand Boulevard, together with the university library and a number of specialist libraries; the National Library, however, is in Buda, in the old Royal Palace.

At present, much research is carried out, not by the universities, but by the Hungarian Academy of Sciences, and applied research is controlled by the respective ministries. Research by enterprises is a neglected area: state industrial firms have not been interested in the introduction of new products, and the results of 'applied' research have rarely been put into practice. Consequently, research establishments occur in the city haphazardly, often in buildings used earlier for other purposes; they are not linked to universities, or to the industrial zones. There is a group of the social science research institutes in the Castle area. At present, plans for a technopol, linked to the territory of the Technical University, is being elaborated.

Of the functions of public health, the big hospitals and specialized health institutions represent the functions of a big city. The statistical data are impressive: there are 31,000 hospital beds in the capital's forty-six hospitals (141 beds per 10,000 inhabitants), 4,100 doctors and 8,800 nurses. In 1987 the hospitals of Budapest processed 638,000 patients, and the average period of treatment was fourteen days. Budapest's basic health care is well staffed: half of Hungary's medical doctors live in Budapest, and 12,000 work in the capital – fifty-eight doctors per 10,000 inhabitants. It should be added that free health care is available for every Hungarian citizen without restriction.

The demographic data presented earlier – such as the high mortality rate, which has been growing for a long time – suggest that the health of the population is poor. Naturally, public health is not wholly to blame: people work in two or three jobs and suffer numerous social tensions; alcoholism is common, and so forth. But the dysfunctions of health care organization are also obvious. In a poor country the state budget cannot give a high level of health care to everybody. The equipment in public health institutions is of a low standard and often out-of-date. A market has developed in high-quality services that is semi-legal. And – in keeping with the logic of state socialism – the functioning of the public health system serves the interests of the service organization rather than the interests of the consumers. Hence, preventive medicine has a lower priority than hospitals, since the latter serve doctors' prestige better. The number of hospital beds is excessively high, but hospitals are quite crowded because patients are kept there too long. Hence, one day of treatment, which is subsidized by the state, is 'cheaper' for the hospitals. The elderly who need nursing are also kept in hospitals, because there are few homes for the aged, and the system of home care is underdeveloped. And finally, after 1945 only one new hospital was built in the capital, though all the old hospitals have been rebuilt and extended by new wings. The hospital network of today is almost as it was at the end of the nineteenth century. The hospitals built then on the outskirts have since been overgrown by the city.

The hospitals are grouped at two points in the city. One is the long line of university hospitals along Üllői Road, an extension of the university district in Pest. The other group is located in the Buda Hills, and was built for the treatment of tuberculosis, a common disease in the first part of the twentieth century. These hospitals have since acquired new functions. The only new hospital was built on the Pest side, in a peripheral district to the south-east.

Commercial functions have always played a great role in the life of the city and have remained important even under the state socialist system – more so than in any other socialist capital. Until recently, foreign trade and wholesale trade was a state monopoly. The headquarters of every foreign trading company and of many wholesale trading companies were in the capital, closely linked to the administrative districts.

In the retail trade, a metropolitan trading centre had developed by the turn of the century, and this has strengthened ever since, representing the strongest commercial space east of Vienna. The main structural elements of this region are the two parallel boulevards around the inner city of Pest, and the two avenues, Andrássy Street and Rákóczi Street – the continuation of Kossuth Lajos Street down to the Budapest Eastern railway station. The latter attracted the big department stores, whereas the medium-sized and medium-level speciality shops are located in the boulevards. In the streets between the governmental and university districts, centring upon Váci Street, there are expensive, high-standard, glamorous, small speciality shops. Many of the streets there have been turned into pedestrian precincts, and the area is a favourite with foreign tourists.

This inner shopping area is also the centre of culture: practically all the theatres, concert halls and the opera are here, as well as galleries, and new and second-hand bookshops, the latter selling rare items at cheap prices. Understandably, this inner area of Pest is lively day and night, though the night life is quieter than that found in West European capitals. These commercial areas embraced the inner residential zones, and five big indoor markets were built here between 1895 and 1897. On the Buda side the main commercial line is Mártírok útja, but it is minor compared to the shopping centre of Pest. In Buda only a single indoor market hall was built: at Batthyány Square, in 1902.

It should be noted that the municipal administration was involved in the food trade. In 1911 the Municipal Food Sales Company was set up with its own bakery, which could sell at lower prices since it bought raw materials directly from the producers. This enabled it to influence retail food prices.

The shopping centre of the inner city did not merely serve the more affluent population. Cheap clothing shops and shops selling industrial products were found around the railway stations and in side streets. The whole city did its shopping – except for everyday groceries – in the inner city. The network of shops became rather scarce in the outer residential zones, where there were mainly food shops and pubs.

State socialism even nationalized trade. The first step was the nationalization of wholesale trade in 1949, and retail trade had been taken over by state enterprises by 1951–2. The restaurants had a similar fate. While private small-scale industry was soon permitted again, though within limitations, decades had to pass for the revival of private retail trade, and even then it often took the form of renting state-owned shops. The revival of private trade only took place in the 1980s. In 1987 there were 5,600 retail shops owned by the state and the co-operatives. 1,000 of these were rented by private individuals, and there were 7,000 privately-owned shops. Of the 3,000 restaurants owned by the state and co-operatives, 1,700 were rented by private entrepreneurs and there were 1,400 privately-owned restaurants. Thus, the private sector had already become dominant in retail trades and catering during the socialist period, which explains the good general supply compared with other socialist countries. This is clearly going to be the economic sector whose privatization will be completed first.

Self-service shops appeared quite early in Budapest, but these have tended to be small, and there are very few supermarkets in the real sense of the term. There are no shopping centres along the roads leading to the capital. But some shopping sub-centres have been built, mainly in the peripheral districts of Kőbánya, Újpest, Óbuda and Kispest. There are no shopping malls and perhaps there will not be in the near future either, as the attraction of the city squares and shopping streets has not decreased. The Hungarian consumer wants to have a food shop, a pub and a café near his or her home. The habits of the Hungarian urban population are nearer to those of the Latin than the Slav peoples: they like to spend time in the public squares of the city, and enjoy informal meetings; they purchase flour, sugar and salt in the supermarket, but like to choose their butcher and greengrocer as a personal acquaintance, and the selection of a baker requires special attention.

State and co-operative trade and catering employs 124,000 people, and the private sector employs about 10–15,000 people. Further expansion of the network of shops can be expected, though the administrative employees of the bureaucracy of the state trading centres will become redundant. (In 1987 there was one administrative member of staff per three manual employees, such as chefs, waiters and assistants.)

Some reference has already been made to the functions of rest and recreation in relation to tourism. The baths, the banks of the Danube, the places of excursion and the museums are used primarily by the inhabitants of Budapest. The green spaces represent an important aspect of this function. The green areas are very extensive: there are 2,925 hectares of woods on the Buda side and 1,487 hectares in Pest, of which 987 hectares are regularly maintained parks. Budapest ranks high in terms of green space among the big cities of Europe. Of regularly maintained parks alone, there are 5 sq.m. per capita. The territorial distribution of green spaces is rather uneven: in the densely-populated inner zones on the Pest side (the Sixth, Seventh and Eighth Districts) there is only 0.22 sq.m. per capita. Beside the Buda forests, the capital has three other extensive green areas. One is the Margaret Island, a green oasis in the heart of the metropolis where there are two swimming pools, sports fields, an open air theatre and two hotels, occupying perhaps rather more than they should of the lovely park with its century-old trees. Fortunately, no cars are allowed on the island any more. The Városliget (City Park) at the end of Andrássy Street around Heroes' Square has an area of 100 hectares with the zoo and fun fair at its edges, offering a different kind of rest and entertainment, mainly to families with children. The third big park is the Népliget (People's Park), which is rather desolate and neglected; its 120 hectares are not utilized. The abundance of green space has made the city rather careless. New building activities carve out space even from the Buda woods. The trees along the roads are being destroyed by air pollution and by the depletion of ground waters.

Functional zones basically reflect the rational use of urban territory – but not only that. The form they take, their monuments and their architectural style, all carry a 'message' about urban society and the spirit of the age. The symbols of the state socialist system have hardly affected the urban landscape. The most spectacular is the Liberation Monument at the top of Gellért Hill. There are a number of monuments dedicated to Soviet soldiers; some statues of Marxist revolutionaries; the parade road near the City Park, the former place of military parades and May Day marches, where used to stand a tribune (a copy of the one in Moscow) where the leaders of the people waved to the parading people (and where Stalin's huge statue stood for three years until the angry Hungarians pulled it down on 23 October 1956); and there is the People's Stadium (every dictatorship builds a stadium). By and large their number is small, and they are scattered throughout the city. Up until the 1960s, the symbols of the previous regime damaged during the war – the Royal Palace, the row of hotels along the Danube, the old ministries and palaces – were not restored. The old National Theatre – a symbol of the nineteenth-century struggles of Hungarian national culture – was sacrificed, perhaps unnecessarily, to the construction of the metro.

The past one-and-a-half decades have seen a growing interest in the Budapest of the turn of the century. The banks of the Danube and the Royal Palace were rebuilt; the post-modern buildings could be easily attached to the buildings of the art nouveau. The style of the shops of the inner city also follows these traditions. The present symbolism of the city passes on the message that this is an old city, a valuable city with a rich past, a Central European city. This is not nostalgia or an idealization of the past, but a modern renewal of the historical roots that have been artificially hacked at.

8
The Budapest agglomeration

The development of the agglomeration zone

Suburbanization – the evolution of the urban agglomeration – is a new phenomenon in the development of Hungarian settlements. It was only around the capital that suburbanization appeared early, around the 1870s. As was mentioned above in the chapter on demography, since 1867 population growth in the suburban zone has always been significantly higher than in Budapest.

The territory of the suburban zone has expanded considerably. The settlements immediately bordering the city were included around 1870. There was unprecedented population growth in this inner belt between 1869 and 1910, when the number of inhabitants grew ten times. The agrarian nature of the villages was transformed, but it did not disappear completely. Population growth was nurtured by three kinds of mobility in addition to natural growth. The first was the emigration of skilled workers from the extremely expensive capital to cheaper places of residence in a rural environment. The second was the significant transfer of industry mainly to the north (Újpest) and to the south-east (Kispest, Pestszenterzsébet), where large tracts of land were available. And the third was immigration from the over-populated agricultural regions of the Great Plain and North Hungary. Migrants from these regions preferred the suburban settlements, not only because they were cheaper, but also because of their rural environment – even if they found work in the capital. These settlements were linked to the capital by trains or trams by the end of the last century. Public transport aided daily commuting and the utilization of the services of Budapest. The establishment of a united Budapest did not stop the expansion of the suburban zone. The capital attracted labour from distances of 20–25 kilometres in the 1930s.

There were several administrative attempts to express the functional relationship of the capital and its environs. A forerunner of these was Act X of 1870, which extended the authority of the Commission of Public Works beyond the limits of the capital 'in the case of certain works'. In 1901 Pest-Pilis-Solt-Kiskun county suggested the amalgamation of some settlements that were already merged into the capital (such as Újpest, Rákospalota, Kispest), but Budapest rejected it at that time. During the inter-war period it was the capital which initiated the creation of Greater Budapest and the delimitation of a broader agglomeration. In 1937 the Act on the settlement and building of the capital stated that 'the Commission of Public Works will elaborate the general and detailed master plan of the capital city of Budapest and its neighbourhood'.

In 1938 a decree of the Minister of the Interior listed six towns and eighteen villages that belonged to the neighbourhood of Budapest; the list was extended by another twenty-one villages in 1941. A broader agglomeration zone was also delineated which included eighty-eight villages. The administrative unification of Budapest and its neighbourhood (Greater Budapest), planned in the 1930s, was accomplished in 1950 (on a territory somewhat smaller than envisaged earlier).

The worker and part-time farmer nature of the zone was retained even at the time of the merger. Thus, in the course of suburbanization around Budapest, the existing agrarian settlements were the first to become those of commuting workers and part-time farmers. At times they became industrial townships. This is how suburbanization began around a number of big West European cities as well; however, the first 'immature' phase dragged on for a very long time in Budapest. In 1971 the border of the Budapest agglomeration was officially set. The 'official' agglomeration did not become a single administrative unit, but rather served the purposes of urban planning. The new outer zone included forty-three settlements (five towns among them) outside Budapest over a territory of 1,143 sq.km., with about 400,000 inhabitants. It was smaller than the territory envisaged by the 1938 draft.

The new delineation was carried out in a simplified way on a demographic basis, as the rapidly growing settlements around the capital were included. Presumably the actual (functional) agglomeration has been larger than the territory delineated, and naturally the regions which provide labour extend much farther, particularly along the railway lines heading south-east and east. In 1980 only 53 per cent of daily commuters came from the 'official' agglomeration.

The relationship between the agglomeration and Budapest is a subject of constant dispute. There is no administrative relationship between them, and not even any co-ordination of local government. There is no joint authority over settlement development. The settlements of the agglomeration belong to Pest county. The chief town of the county is Budapest, which is also the national capital. It therefore enjoys a special administrative status – it does not belong to the county. The agglomeration zone is overcrowded. Its population keeps on growing even today, while that of the country as a whole is decreasing, and the local authorities are unable to supply, or easily to integrate, the in-migrants attracted by the labour hunger of the capital. The local authorities in the agglomeration jealously guard their autonomy and are reluctant to associate themselves with the capital. The memory of 1950 is still alive, when Budapest forcibly swallowed the settlements of the inner agglomeration zone against their will. In the mean time the capital complains that the inhabitants of the agglomeration massively utilize those public services which are maintained by the money of Budapest taxpayers (and, of course, by huge subsidies).

In the course of its 100 years of expansion, the Budapest agglomeration usually swallowed agrarian settlements, which became part-time farmer and subsequently blue-collar settlements. A sizeable manufacturing industry developed in some places in the agglomeration, promoting their growth into labour suburbs. The blue-collar characteristics dominate even today. There are few new suburban settlements – new in the sense that they have not grown out of the extension of the old villages. Estates of rented flats have been built in only a few places. With the subdivision of some holdings in the first decades of the century, garden cities have developed (for instance Érd, which has grown into a town). Another new phenomenon is the white-collar middle-class suburb. Settlements such as Szentendre and Leányfalu are located along the Danube in attractive settings. Here, some former holiday districts have been transformed into quality residential areas.

This 'delay' of the agglomeration of Budapest is due to a number of factors: the relative weakness of the middle classes, their unfavourable financial position, the unusually strong industrial nature of the city, the survival of the residential prestige of the city centre, and finally, the over-bound nature of the city as a consequence of the administrative reform of 1950. As a result, suburbanization has taken place within the administrative borders of the city: for instance, the white-collar suburbs have developed in the former recreation districts on the Buda side.

Five phases can be distinguished in the evolution of the Budapest agglomeration. In the first phase (1870–1900), rapid industrialization created industrial suburbs. Their land requirements made many industries seek locations on cheap plots outside the borders of the city, and usually they settled their workers around the factories. The industrial establishments – and hence the first industrial villages – evolved along the Danube, to the north and south of the city. In the second phase (1900–20) the industry of the inner suburban zone expanded considerably and employed 40 per cent of the industrial workforce in the agglomeration. In 1910 three of the five largest industrial cities of Hungary belonged to the agglomeration! Commuting began as public transport developed. (In 1910, 15,000 workers commuted to the capital and the industrial suburbs from the more distant villages.) The third phase (1920–45) resulted in the further expansion of the suburban zone, both in territory – mainly over to Buda and in its functions – which now embraced intensive agriculture, and recreation as well. The fourth phase (1945–75) brought about the already-mentioned administrative merger of the inner zone and the further expansion of industry, with the partial relocation of industry out of the capital. Agriculture has retreated, and the residential areas have expanded, making it the main function of some suburban settlements. Smaller local centres (satellite cities) have also appeared in the agglomeration. The fifth phase has been the post-industrial development of the agglomeration. The inhabitants of Budapest increasingly move out of the city, and the industrial character of the agglomeration is being reduced; hence, commuting by industrial labour is also decreasing.

Functions of the agglomeration zone

Budapest and the settlements of the agglomeration zone constitute a single, large functional spatial organization. The functions of the suburbs have developed mainly in relation to Budapest. However, they do not depend totally upon the capital; they have an autonomous life of their own, and their autonomy may even grow after the establishment of the new local authorities.

It is difficult to place the functions in order of significance. Presumably the most important is the residential function, as 400,000 people live in the suburbs, one-sixth of the total metropolitan population. This proportion shows that the centre of gravity of the population has not yet really shifted to the suburbs, partly because public transport is inadequately developed. The majority of the population live in rural communities, in family houses with gardens. Two-thirds of the population (three-quarters of industrial workers) go to work in other communities (mainly in the capital) daily. (Eleven of the thirty-eight rural communities have more than 10,000 inhabitants each.) Immigrants arriving in the suburbs can find accommodation only with difficulty. The large rural settlements are quite disorderly and grow spontaneously, while the infrastructure is poor. Since the division of plots has progressed haltingly (because only land owned by the state is available), planning permission is often not sought for building work. Few flats are available within the agglomeration; consequently, unskilled labour from distant regions often live as sub-tenants under crowded, poor housing conditions.

The industrial functions of the agglomeration zone are also worth mentioning, since industry employs almost 40,000 people. Industry has been set up in different phases and forms in the agglomeration. Manufacturing industry has not been totally scattered; large and small industrial centres have developed, mainly along the Danube and the main railway lines, but mostly on the left bank of the river. Only eleven of the forty-three settlements of the agglomeration have more than 1,000 industrial jobs, and these employ 78 per cent of industrial wage-earners.

Some important industries were set up in the outer agglomeration zone before World War II demanding either space or labour (the textile industry). In the wave of industrialization of 1950–70 (strongly limited after 1965):

- Some major state investments were completed (such as the Csepel Car Factory at Szigetszentmiklós and the Danube Oil Refinery at Százhalombatta).
- Some factories were forced to move out of the capital because of town planning or environmental protection regulations. (In 1959 all the capital's industrial estates were classified under three headings by the municipal council: (a) may be developed and expanded; (b) may be maintained at its present dimensions; (c) should be removed from the capital. Relocation was subsidized by the government.)
- The Budapest companies willingly transferred some of their less modern units to the country where cheap, less skilled labour was abundantly available. The first wave of such transfers remained in the vicinity of the capital (in the second half of the 1960s), and tried to utilize the still free labour of the agglomeration. Transfers to the more distant regions followed later. Enterprise headquarters in the capital primarily retained management, the R&D divisions, and the production of new, up-to-date goods. This is indicated by the fact that, while only 59 per cent of industry employees in Budapest were manual workers in 1987, the figure was 69 per cent in the industry of the suburban zone.

The industrial functions of the suburban zone are not very significant. Industry employs altogether 20,000 people in the towns of the 'official' agglomeration, and 39,000 in the whole. The majority of blue-collar workers commute. Not all of them go to Budapest, as there is cross-commuting also within the zone. Outside the official agglomeration, but functionally within it, there are two industrially advanced towns, Gödöllő and Vác. They attract labour from some settlements of the agglomeration as well.

In the 1970s restrictions were imposed on the opening of new industrial estates in the capital and in its neighbourhood in order to slow down the population growth of the agglomeration. A general ban on the establishment of new manufacturing firms was announced, and only the central government was authorized to make exceptions – rather than the Ministry of Building and Urban Development, under whose powers it would properly have come. In theory, only industries directly serving the agglomeration (such as waste incinerators) were to be exempted from the ban. In practice, however, the pressure of the industrial lobby brought results, so that the largest petro-chemical combine of the country was built in the agglomeration (Százhalombatta). Several polluting factories were transferred from the capital to the agglomeration, and environmental concern is now beginning to be expressed by the population. The expansion of industrial jobs continued right into the 1970s (in Budapest the number of those employed in industry has been decreasing since 1964), but a decline has set in here too in the 1980s.

It is estimated that private service industries have grown rapidly in the suburban zone, where it is easier to acquire plots than in the capital. Unfortunately, statistics still contain information only on so-called 'socialist' industry (state and co-operative industries), so little is known about the apparently dynamic private sector.

Agricultural functions have naturally declined sharply in importance. The Budapest market had earlier encouraged intensive cultivation in the vicinity of the capital. In the 1930s, 60 per cent of fresh vegetables on the Budapest market came from the suburbs, and dairy production was also significant. Fresh, untreated milk fetched a good price in the Budapest market, so that some dairy farms survived in isolation even within the built-up parts of the city. The character of agriculture has undergone great changes. Cattle breeding has practically disappeared, but the breeding of poultry and rabbits is still widespread in blue-collar households. Suburban houses are mostly surrounded by large and intensively-farmed gardens. These gardens yield a large quantity of eggs and fruit for the Budapest market even today. The vegetable supply from the suburban zone is insignificant, but the production of mushrooms, flowers and ornamental plants has increased considerably.

Fourteen large agricultural producers' co-operatives operate within the agglomeration in addition to numerous smaller farms. They are well provided with capital, thanks to their mostly non-agricultural activities. Only a quarter of their gross production income comes from agriculture. They have many industrial and servicing activities and display an excellent entrepreneurial spirit, profiting from the inflexibility of the oversized large-scale industries run by the state. Presumably their industrial and commercial sections will be privatized and separated off from the agricultural co-operatives. The agricultural co-operatives have cultivated their fields quite extensively. The profit earned from their industrial and service activities (far larger than that from their agricultural work) has partly been invested in the development of certain highly intensive branches (flower growing, biotechnology).

Agriculture, despite its marked decline, continues to be more significant in Budapest than in agglomerations in the West. The farms own 47,000 hectares of rather low quality land, 90 per cent of which is cultivated. This arises from the special social structure of the agglomeration zone (a lot of in-migrants come from distant agricultural regions), but it is also due to the fact that there is a good market for food products, that the custom of consuming fresh vegetables and fruit survives (despite the higher prices), and that large-scale farming has refused to engage in intensive cultivation.

The holiday and recreation functions have gained in importance. Here the Danube plays a major role. These functions offer an increasing number of jobs in the agglomeration. They can be classified in three groups: (a) international and national tourism; (b) excursion tourism; and (c) second homes.

Budapest is a major centre of international tourism. Turnover shows relatively little seasonal change (whereas the tourist season of the other large centre, Lake Balaton, in only three months). Tourism in the capital is now beginning to extend over the agglomeration. There are few large hotels outside the capital, but the number of small private guesthouses and boarding-houses has been rapidly increasing. The renting of rooms is widespread. This kind of tourism dominates the right bank of the Danube north of Budapest, and the Danube Bend almost exclusively. There is still plenty of unrealized potential: for instance, the potential for hotel development on the main roads out from Budapest. What Hungary cannot offer in terms of accommodation is relatively cheap family hotels, and there is little opportunity for such developments in the inner areas of the city.

If the much-debated Budapest Expo World Fair is realized in 1996, the southern part of the agglomeration would definitely benefit. (Initially it was planned as a joint project with Vienna, but after Vienna's surprise referendum result, which voted against the Expo, the chances of Budapest going it alone look increasingly slim.) This event would bring a sudden growth in tourism: it would require a massive construction of hotels for a single occasion, but would ensure the further growth of Northern Italian, Austrian and German tourism that had already begun in 1990. The larger hotels have tended to be used by business people and tourist groups (the average stay is less than three days), whereas private accommodation is taken up by families of more modest means coming for their holidays (average stay of nine days). Conditions are favourable for the expansion of tourism and for the spread of small private accommodation in the agglomeration, primarily in the already fashionable Danube Bend, in the Buda Hills and in the Ráckeve section of the

Danube that is yet to be discovered (south of Budapest).

The main targets of excursion tourism are the regions already listed above. Tourists staying in Budapest gladly spend a day in the picturesque Danube Bend. The building of the Nagymaros dam, significantly damaging to the natural environment of the Danube Bend, was suspended by the government at an early phase of construction in response to the massive popular protest (restoring the land to its original state will be expensive).

The Buda Hills and those of the Danube Bend are pleasant wooded regions near the capital which attract a large number of hikers in every season of the year. The extensive forests are carefully managed parks, and a large part of them are protected areas. Timber production has stopped, and the forests now serve mainly recreational purposes. Dobogókő, 35 km. from Budapest, is an excellent winter skiing resort, and ski tracks can also be found within the borders of the capital, though there is not always enough snow for skiing every year.

The river bank immediately north of Budapest (and within the city as well) is excellent for aquatic sports. This is the site of Aquincum, the capital of the Roman province, and the name of this stretch of the right bank of the river – Roman Bank – recalls its history. Water sports have declined since World War II, though there is great potential. Today the region is neglected, the nationalized boat-houses are not maintained properly, and the attractiveness of the Danube has been greatly diminished because no bathing is possible in its polluted waters.

The zone of privately-owned second homes is very extensive in the Budapest agglomeration. In this respect, the most important parts are the regions along the right side of the Danube, but segments of the zone can be found practically all over the suburban belt, either linked to the inner parts of settlements, or in separate areas. The owners come from the most diverse social classes. Blue-collar owners have mostly purchased plots in the south and south-east in the proximity of the industrial zones (where they were cheaper), where they intensively cultivate their gardens. The Ráckeve branch of the Danube has been occupied by anglers. The building regulations of the settlements along the right side of the Danube attract more affluent owners.

A survey of second homes in Szentendre has shown that the owners were almost exclusively inhabitants of Budapest, and their permanent residence – as could be expected – was located either in the inner residential zone of Budapest, or in the new housing estates. A large proportion of owners lived in state flats. As a large number of second homes are located near Budapest, and their owners often make their way out by public transport, the urban residential zone is effectively doubled. In summer the owners often live in their second homes for months, even though the various building restrictions have allowed for small living spaces, and the plots are often without drainage systems, telephones, and so forth. The large number of second homes is a partial correction of the anomalies of centrally planned and managed urbanization, at the cost of great human effort and waste of resources. Many owners would prefer to live in a family house with a garden, or in a flat with better living conditions. They could even have afforded it, but were not able to satisfy their needs because of the lack of, or the distorted character of, the housing market. Socialist urban development preferred large, homogenous housing estates, as described above, so that citizens of above-average needs but of not particularly abundant means could not find a suitable home for themselves (and they could not pay the forbidding price of the villas of the Buda Hills). Finance experts realized towards the end of the 1960s that the accumulation of the population's surplus money exercised an inflationary pressure, so the government permitted the purchase of plots and the building of weekend houses. Socialist principles also had to be given their due: the land, which had been originally owned by the state or by co-operatives, was divided up into smaller plots, and was given out only for 'lasting usage' (the right to use it could even be inherited). Building regulations hindered the construction of houses for permanent residence in these recreation zones. Hence, savings could be made in the development of a fully-fledged infrastructure. In addition, only one such property was permitted per family. Now the second homes have become private property, and restrictions of ownership have been abolished, but many unnecessary second homes have already been built. If the owners had had the opportunity to purchase a plot supplied with public utilities in the first place when the land was being divided, then they could have built a permanent home there, so that their flat in a housing estate would have been freed for the next family on the waiting list. The 'savings' made in building housing estates has led to a waste of space, money, and human energy that have been invested in the building of second homes and the later introduction of public utilities.

Some settlements in the suburban zone have certain functions as local centres. The zone is both attached to Budapest, and has a network of small towns of its own. These settlements are small and medium-sized towns, and their role is growing within the zone. This is where the industrial and servicing functions are concentrated, and where a significant proportion of population growth is attracted. The ten cities are (with population in thousands in 1990): Budaörs, 19.8; Dunakeszi, 26.1; Érd, 43.3; Gödöllő, 28.2; Monor, 18.4; Ráckeve, 8.1; Százhalombatta, 16.5; Szentendre, 19.4; Szigetszentmiklós, 19.4 and Vác, 34.0. They can be classified into different types by their origin and role. Szentendre and Vác are the only old cities among them. Vác, with 34,000 inhabitants, is an important town: it is an episcopal seat, an educational and health centre, and has considerable industry as well. Forte, the only photographic paper and film manufacturing firm, and the large cement factory near the city are of particular significance, but communications technology, electronics and clothing industries should also be mentioned. The historic significance of the city, partly due to its favourable location (on the Danube) for transport, is attested by the eighteenth-century baroque parts of the town. The first Hungarian railway line was opened between Pest and Vác in 1843.

Szentendre lies on the opposite bank of the Danube, although it is separated from Vác by the long Szentendre island. This lovely town is a favourite destination of excursion tourism. A town of art galleries, churches and museums, it draws a cultural colourfulness from the ethnic mix of its population. The town is only 15 kilometres from Budapest, and it is a favourite spot for intellectuals moving out from the capital.

The other towns are young products of the rapid growth of the past few decades. Of these, Gödöllő has the most complex functions. It is the most important centre of Hungarian agricultural research and higher education; several agricultural research institutes and experimental farms are located here, besides the University of Agricultural Sciences. Nor are the town's industries insignificant. In the past it was a royal hunting-seat, and the Austro-Hungarian emperor regularly stayed here.

The three cities of Dunakeszi, Százhalombatta and Szigetszentmiklós owe their existence to industrialization. Százhalombatta is the terminal of the oil pipeline coming from the Soviet Union. The largest refinery of the country and a power station are operated here. Szigetszentmiklós is the town of the Csepel Car Works. Dunakeszi's functions are residential and industrial. Budaörs, Érd and Monor are commuting villages that have expanded. Ráckeve, on the southern edge of the agglomeration, is a traditional small town.

Three of the towns in the agglomeration (Monor, Ráckeve and Vác) have witnessed a fall in population. The losses caused by migration were aggravated by a natural decrease in Monor and Ráckeve. Significant migrational gains have only been achieved by Budaörs and Szentendre, the two communities favoured by those leaving Budapest. The highest growth (16 per cent) has been experienced in the young industrial town of Százhalombatta, where natural growth has also been high (8 per 1,000 per year), a rare phenomenon in Hungary.

The special features of the Budapest agglomeration

The Budapest agglomeration has several special features when compared with West European urban agglomerations. They basically derive from the fact that the development of the agglomeration was stranded in its first phase, though its beginning was by no means belated. The post-World War II economic development considerably increased the territory and population of the agglomeration zone, but its social structure was not modernized. The state socialist period preserved the blue-collar and part-time farmer character of the agglomeration.

The most important feature of the agglomeration is its social structure. A main feature is the high proportion of poorly qualified semi-skilled and unskilled labourers, especially in the south-east. In the blue-collar suburbs, in-migrants come mainly from the north-eastern parts of the country, which are the most backward agrarian regions still suffering from agrarian over-population. Immigrants often settle down in the same street of the suburb, or work near one another in Budapest, and are definitely engaged in auxiliary production. These places of residence have low social prestige; members of mobile social groups seek to move to Budapest or to the 'better' suburbs – moving into the city still has attractions. Those local centres of the agglomeration with local industries are the better suburbs, and here we find skilled workers and technical intellectuals living.

White-collar emigration is not yet extensive, but it is growing. Its main destinations include the villages and small towns in the hills along the right side of the Danube. Some of those who leave the capital belong to the upper middle classes and seek the attractive natural environment. Others are highly qualified but badly paid intellectuals, who are unable to pay for a flat suiting their needs in Budapest. Large-scale population changes have occurred in these villages: a considerable part of their population has been Germans who were partly deported in 1946–7. A large part of the new settlers (prior to the appearance of the intellectuals from Budapest) were white-collar or qualified intellectuals from distant regions who were attracted by the environment and were looking for a different kind of suburb from those their uneducated kin were moving to.

The introduction of a market economy will presumably cause significant changes in the suburban zone. In the centre of the capital, the market will push up property prices massively, and it will be dominated by business centres, banks and luxury shops, and the hitherto rudimentary Central Business District will develop there. This can be expected primarily in the decayed inner residential zone of the Pest side, and the signs are already there that this will happen. This will force out the residential zones, units such as stores, printing presses and repair workshops that do not make intensive use of space, and even some of the state and municipal offices. Office space decentralization, the proportions of which are as yet unknown, will affect the Budapest agglomeration as well: offices with a small number of clients will appear in the housing estates at the periphery of the city and in the suburbs.

The suburban residential zone will be extended and partly rebuilt, and emigration from the capital will grow. The difference between the suburban settlements receiving middle-class and rural immigrants may become even more marked. Presumably the agglomeration zone may further extend and the peripheral villages will receive the rural immigrants, but large masses of immigrants cannot be expected as the population of the country has been decreasing for quite some time. The future of rural employment cannot be assessed yet, but significant rural unemployment can be envisaged. Those who are forced to migrate may mainly hope to find (but not necessarily get) jobs in Budapest, since country towns, with their imbalanced industrialization, will also be suffering structural unemployment.

Foreign migrant workers may turn up among the in-migrants. At present there is a large number – more than 100,000 according to some estimates – of illegal immigrants in the country who have come mainly from the Balkans (Romania, Bulgaria and Turkey), and from Poland. Though the majority try to cross the Austrian border illegally, presumably some of them will ultimately obtain a residence permit, or will take up jobs in the 'black' economy.

Private enterprise will enjoy a boom in the suburban zone. Less capital is needed than in Budapest. The economic relations between the capital and its immediate vicinity may become multifaceted. The question arises as to how the coexistence of Budapest and its agglomeration will function. The strict command economy was unable to co-ordinate the functioning of the co-existing groups of settlements. Though a settlement plan was elaborated for the entire agglomeration, it remained a planner's dreams. Co-operation may be based on the voluntary association of the new local authorities, although at present rivalry is stronger than solidarity between the neighbouring settlements. When the fate of the settlements depended on the bureaucratic redistribution of the budget by central government, the administrative heads of the settlements struggled against each other for the benevolence of the centre. Presumably the freely-elected local authorities will at first turn inwards and deal with their internal problems, while suspiciously eyeing the large city in the centre of the agglomeration which used to wield its central power oppressively.

The long and excessive dominance of industrialization has made the transfer to the post-industrial phase difficult and has produced special features in the development of the agglomeration in the 1980s. The general growth of the suburbs has been halted and has become geographically highly differentiated. Between 1980 and 1990, out of the thirty-eight settlements of the suburban zone, the population grew only in fifteen, and it fell in twenty-three. This decline occurred mainly in the residential blue-collar communities. In Budapest, industrial jobs have fallen significantly (by 300,000 between 1970 and 1990), but the fall in industrial occupations has begun in the suburban zone too. This is in part a natural process, the result of the surge of jobs in the tertiary occupations, but it is also related to the economic crisis of the country. In fact, the decline in industrial jobs is caused not so much by the technological renewal of industry, as by its general decline. The tertiary sector has not spread sufficiently in the current difficult economic situation; some of the unqualified commuting workers doing heavy manual jobs have been made redundant. The number of industrial workers commuting daily to Budapest has dropped by 21 per cent during the past decade. As a consequence of a minor demographic peak at the turn of the 1960s and 1970s, the labour resources of Budapest itself have temporarily grown. The population aged between 20 and 24 entering the workforce is hardly any less than the number of those going into retirement.

Rootless migrant workers from distant regions and living as subtenants are leaving the rural suburban settlements that were swelled by the earlier industrial boom, as are some of the children of those who came in the 1960s. Where are they going? Are they returning to their birthplace? Do the better-educated try to go to Budapest? We do not have this information yet. But the constant growth of the agglomeration zone, which has been going on for more than a century, has stopped. Growth can be found primarily in those pleasant settlements on the right side of the Danube where inhabitants of the capital would willingly move to; this has been the source of the increasing suburban-zone population. The inflow of unskilled rural labour is being replaced by the outflow of the middle classes of Budapest. It would be even more marked had the suburban zone not been annexed to Budapest in 1950. During the past decade, the population has grown in only six of the twenty-two districts of Budapest; all six used to be autonomous suburban settlements before 1950.

Part Four

Plans and planners

9
The history of urban planning

The development of modern urban planning

The need for regulated urban growth first arose in Budapest in the early eighteenth century. This is the time of the first survey of Budapest. Parts of the city walls were pulled down, and the streets began to be paved with limestone and maintained. Documents from the reign of Maria Theresa (1740–1780) show that permission for construction had to be sought from the Municipality of Pest. The Municipality distributed free plots along the city walls during the course of its land settlement activities, where construction and agricultural cultivation began. Willows were planted in 1755 on the marshy lands of the future Városliget (City Park) and the Lipótváros. In the Tabán district at the foot of Castle Hill, house plots were allocated to about 600 families.

The physical planning of the period was not significant. The basis of the medieval urban structure was not modified, and the existing network of streets was left untouched. There did not yet exist in the baroque period those bourgeois forces demanding rapid urban development and a redistribution of the physical and urban conditions. The criteria used to interfere in changes in territorial processes were settlement and social policy, rather than town plans or building regulations.

By the end of the eighteenth century, the Treasury administration of the Court was entrusted with urban settlement and architecture. The Treasury set to work with great ambitions: it announced that the city needed a casino, a festival hall and a theatre. But the rather conservative magistrate of Pest protested against these ideas in several petitions.

At this time comprehensive architectural regulations were issued for Pest, and construction was subject to licensing. The Emperor issued a number of taxation decrees related to urban planning. He reduced taxes for those who started building work, and citizenship was granted to those who built their own houses. A number of such ideas and plans were born which still significantly influence the landscape of the city. The plans of the present Deák Square, Erzsébet Square and Bajcsy-Zsilinszky Street were prepared at that time.

The flood of 1795 and the damage it caused in Pest required new intervention in urban planning. The issues of the Danube flood control and the shortages of transport and public utilities were raised loudly. Any solution, however, demanded not only a conception of urban planning that went beyond mere regulations, but more particularly, funding.

The activities of Joseph, the palatine of Hungary (1776–1847), son of Leopold II, the Hungarian King, were of outstanding importance. During his fifty-four-year rule in Hungary he sought a solution to the city's technical problems, and to this end had the general settlement plan of Pest drawn up. The architect János Hild played a major role in the plan, which was completed in 1804, and he brought his commitment to Classicism from Vienna. The so-called Hild plan concentrated mainly on the settlement of the inner, historical kernel of the city and on the development of an adjacent imposing district which was to be called Lipótváros (Leopold Town). It was at this time that Joseph Square, Gisella Square (the present Vörösmarty Square), and the Classicist row of houses lining the Pest bank of the Danube were built on the basis of the plan. The measures included in the plan, besides the regulatory ideas, made it especially important. It also set the aim of parcelling out the outlying areas. The palatine set up the so-called Improvement Commission as well, which was the first professional planning body.

The Improvement Commission, which directed public as well as private construction, was independent of the municipality, subordinate only to the Council of Governor-General with funds obtained from various taxes, duties and bank loans. As a result of its work, a Classicist city with Hungarian features was created.

The first permanent bridge, the Chain Bridge, was built between 1842 and 1849 in the spirit of Classicism, upon Count István Széchenyi's recommendation. Széchenyi was the first statesman to see the city as the capital of the country. It was he who suggested the name Budapest. In the 1830s and 1840s, Széchenyi played a major role in making Pest and Buda the heart of the country; he had the idea of locating the Houses of Parliament on the bank of the Danube, and the foundation of the Academy of Sciences, the casino, the horse races and the Technical University were also associated with his name. However, after the collapse of the Hungarian War of Independence of 1848–9, the Commission and the urban planning of Pest were temporarily wound up owing to increased Austrian centralization.

The history of urban planning in Budapest is closely related to the centralizing efforts of the Habsburgs, and also with the attempts of Hungary to separate and form a nation-state. Whenever the intervention of the central authorities weakened and allowed Hungarian autonomy to grow, there was greater opportunity for expressing territorial and urban interests and for the co-ordination of the concerns of central and local urban planning. This was particularly so during the second part of the nineteenth century, when relations within the Habsburg empire, Hungary's new bargaining position, and internal power relations offered good opportunities for the representation of the interests of the capital.

In the 1850s, Vienna, Paris and London underwent extensive development. The world fairs of the period were evidence of their openness towards the whole world and of the successes of modern urban development. Budapest, however, still did not have a comprehensive settlement concept, and since there was no adequate professional apparatus, the magistrates of the city lacked the necessary expertise. The Hungarian government, in rivalry with Austria and Vienna, needed to create a big European city through the merger of the three towns. It not only wanted the demonstrative effect of the merger, but also sought to show the power of the central Hungarian authorities in its intervention in the large-scale planning of the city. For these reasons the Hungarian government decided to establish a comprehensive planning authority in the form of the Municipal Commission of Public Works.

The Commission of Public Works was a body 'both above and beside' the capital (Siklóssy, 1931, p. 9). The members of the Commission were delegated by both the government and the cities of Pest and Buda on the basis of their expertise. The ex officio chairman of the Commission of Public Works was the Hungarian Prime Minister. Thus, the Hungarian government safeguarded the control and supervision of the Commission. In contrast to earlier practice, the delegates of the authorities of Pest and Buda were also given an opportunity to participate in planning and in the representation of the interests of the city.

The parliamentary disputes of the day, particularly in the early period, suggest that many concerns were expressed on behalf of the city: many people thought that the new settlement authority would be yet another agency of central intervention which would further weaken the autonomy of the city. Others, in particular the reform politicians, saw it as the strengthening of urban autonomy. The Commission of Public Works undoubtedly expressed the centralizing efforts of the Hungarian government. And it was inevitably detrimental to certain local urban interests. However, the activities of the Commission of Public Works constitute one of the most significant periods in the history of the city. It was this body which prepared the merger of the towns, which was essential to the concept of a comprehensive plan. The division of the three cities had hindered uniform development for a long time. This is indicted by the fact that the council of Buda suggested the merger as early as 1848, but in the political situation of the time this was rejected by the empire. During the period after the defeat in the 1848–9 War of Independence, only the cities of Old Buda and Buda were united. Presumably the intention was to block any development of a metropolitan city which could compete with Vienna and strengthen the Hungarian government.

The Commission of Public Works was given control over urban investments and the implementation of regulations by the government. The structure of the road and street network of the city was developed between 1870 and the turn of the century. The first avenue, Andrássy Street, was built between 1871 and 1878, and the development of the system of boulevards was begun at the same time. By 1886 the Inner Boulevard was completed. The Grand Boulevard was opened in 1896 during the millennial celebrations of the existence of Hungary. In the same year the second underground railway in Europe was opened. In 1870 the decision was made to establish the City Park for the leisure and recreation of the inhabitants. In 1880, the race-course, attached to the City Park, was completed, as was Stefánia Row running across the Park in 1882. The artesian wells of the City Park were developed between 1868 and 1878, thus laying the foundations of medicinal spas.

City planning was permeated by the idea of order, when the roads and streets were traced, the height of buildings set, and palaces and pairs of fountains were built in an identical style. The same idea can be found in every big city of the period. International influence is not only indicated by the idea of order, but also by the construction manual that was produced at the time, which followed the pattern of other European cities. The manual divided the city into zones and set the width of streets and pavements. Factories with unpleasant effects had to be located in suburban areas. The manual established certain conditions of zonal social differences, in order to define the different interests of the city centre and the inner districts, the outer areas and the Buda Hills.

One feature of the various interventions was the concept of breaking away from the past. As a consequence, historical monuments were unfortunately damaged, particularly in the historical kernel of the city and Buda's Castle Hill. Although the main interventions were concentrated in the areas outside the old city walls of Pest, attention was also paid to the historic city centre. The remodelling of the city centre was started in the 1890s. Here, the idea of order could only be applied with difficulty. The policy towards plots had made them expensive and hard to expropriate. The district was overcrowded because of the population inflow. The streets were irregular and narrow, there were few squares and little room for construction.

The regulation of the Buda Castle and city was prepared at the turn of the century. The foundation stone of the reconstruction of the Royal Palace was laid by the King in 1896, on the occasion of the millennial celebrations. But construction work on the Castle was accelerated only after the turn of the century, turning it into a stately quarter. It replaced its fortress character with a worthy royal palace, but it also removed numerous monuments, including several delightful medieval buildings and all the old city gates with the exception of the Vienna Gate.

The Commission of Public Works did not work under at all favourable conditions while tackling this massive task. It still was without a well-trained apparatus of experts, and its financial opportunities were limited. In comparison to Vienna, the Hungarian capital was in a particularly difficult position, for while the Austrian capital received extensive plots of land free of charge from the Emperor for the development of squares and parks, the citizens of Budapest had to pay huge amounts, for the plots and hundreds of houses had to be expropriated. The sharp conflicts of interest between the capital and the government caused additional problems. But the first period was characterized by optimism and the euphoria following the Compromise. The problems emerged only later. László Siklóssy's book relates that 'when the struggle for the development of the capital was launched under the leadership of the Commission of Public Works, everybody had the vision of an airy, modern city of palaces with broad streets' (Siklóssy, 1931, p. 326). However, the real processes raised an increasing number of problems, and not only because a large number of crowded tenement blocks were built in the wake of speculation with the plots, which contrasted with the idea of a city of palaces. A number of conflicting interests flared up around planning. There were increasing signs of a crisis in the integrating mechanisms; too many interests were left out of planning.

Planning always represents the interests of some social group, and if it does not stand for the central authorities, then it manifests strong group interests for one reason or another. In this case the interests represented were those of entrepreneurial capital, which hoped for large capital returns from the building of tenement houses, villas and palaces. These entrepreneurial interests did not exclude the residential demands of the former aristocracy and the upper circles of the *grand bourgeoisie*. The elegant palaces built beside the tenement houses, the villa districts, and the institutions and infrastructure serving comfort and culture unambiguously satisfied the life expectations of the latter, while also guaranteeing the profit of the former.

The social groups that were squeezed out of the benefits of city planning were primarily those which lived in the outer districts and the suburban regions of the city. The interventions and different kinds of construction mainly covered the inner areas, while the suburbs remained largely neglected. The *petit bourgeois* and more qualified worker strata, who would willingly have undertaken the building of their own homes, were also left out of the integrative processes of planning, for the prescribed breadth of plots did not allow for such kinds of construction in the inner parts of the city. The regulations only permitted the building of family houses for people with good incomes; the municipal authorities did not issue permits for the construction of smaller houses.

The representatives of those interests that were not benefiting demanded with growing vigour that the interest representation of city planning should be restructured. Part of the criticism was worded in terms of the difficulties that restricted the extensive development of the city. They declared that the resistance of the city authorities to the growing inflow was wrong, and they proposed that tenement blocks on the English pattern should be built in Budapest, which would give even the poorest groups the chance to move into the city centre. At present, the argument ran, these strata are moving to the outlying settlements of the city, living under very poor conditions. A number of proposals were made that the city regulations should offer an opportunity for the development of smaller houses and plots in the inner areas, and large villas and palaces should be built only along the avenues, thus allowing the construction of houses by people with less money.

Another focus of contemporary criticism, based in part on social considerations, was the acceleration of extensive urban development. It held that the situation of the poorer social strata, who were left out of the integrative processes of city planning, were not solved by the building of tenement houses in the inner areas, partly because of the constant rent rises and partly because environmental hazards were a strong feature of those districts. The garden cities built in the outer zones, and the privately-owned family houses, offered greater social protection to these groups, and greater guarantee for the regulation of city development.

However, these criticisms were not heeded. The city policy of 1894 continued to regard the outer territories as zones for uniform tenement blocks, and to lay down large plot sizes. The building of family houses by lower status groups was thus blocked. These families moved to the peripheral settlements offering the cheapest accommodation. Therefore, the first suburbs were of a working-class nature, but with more advantageous conditions than in the inner residential zone of the city. As a result, the inequality of the inner parts of the capital and the difference in development between the inner and outer districts survived for a very long time. Building in the transitory zone slowed down, and only in the 1920s did the bourgeois middle classes start to build family houses. However, the poorer social groups were still left out of the integrative processes of urban policy and planning.

Some Hungarian experts believe the city authorities had no overall conception about changes in spatial processes. However, it is more probable that the processes at work arose from the requirements of the given phase of urbanization, and furthermore, from the requirements of the power relations. The planning of the period, the relative autonomy of the capital, the limited resources which could be spent on planning, and the integrated interest relations could only lead to the uneven development of the larger units of the city.

The situation that evolved underwent slight changes after World War I. Planning became increasingly autonomous and dynamic in the capital. This was made possible by the fact that, by that time, only two authorities were dealing with planning: the Commission of Public Works and the municipality of the capital, which were not only more dynamic, but represented the already more advanced principles of urban planning. First of all, efforts were made to limit speculation in plots, especially in the inner districts. As a result, speculators purchased plots in the suburban settlements of the capital, divided them up and sold them off. Massive expropriation campaigns were launched. Private construction works were encouraged by the money obtained, both this way and by various favourable tax measures, to build following the latest styles of modern city building. This period saw the development of Újlipótváros (New Leopold Town), with modern flats built around gardens and courtyards. The minimum plot size was reduced in the 1920s and 1930s, and as a result the strengthened bourgeois middle strata started the vigorous construction of family houses in the intermediate zone.

The new processes did not change the outlook for the lower status groups. They either could not get into the inner areas, or were increasingly squeezed out to the peripheral settlements where they bought cheap plots without public amenities for their houses. This strategy suited the administrators of the peripheral districts as well, who were happy to divide up a large part of their land and sell it to property agents, creating income to boost their budgets. The agents did not develop public amenities either, as they were looking to sell the plots off for a quick profit. These settlements were merged with Budapest in 1950.

The city planning mechanisms of the inter-war period did not essentially change the broader spatial and social processes which had unfolded during the previous period. The territorial inequalities persisted; the groups with capital and property preserved their advantageous position; those who missed out remained in a socially disadvantaged position; and the process of suburbanization continued. While in the majority of large western cities it was the wealthier middle and upper middle classes who moved to the suburbs, in Budapest the upper middle classes either remained in the inner districts of the city, or moved to the green zones of Buda which did not constitute a continuous belt in the 1930s. The middle and lower middle classes could be found in the outer districts, but they came not from the inner parts of the city, but from other settlements or the mostly blue-collar suburbs.

Plans and planners

In contrast to Western European practice, no effort was made to treat the spatial and social tensions or the conflicting interests which had evolved over time. Communist planning after World War II made such promises ideologically, the results of which will be seen below.

Urban planning under state socialism

The initial situation

In 1945, young experts joined the Commission of Public Works. A number of them were advocates of modern architecture, and some had been members of the Hungarian CIAM group, who tried to alter the imbalances of the city. It was upon their recommendation that the Commission of Public Works decided to modify the 1940 city development plan. In July that year a committee was set up to prepare an urban development plan. The report, entitled 'The uniform development of Greater Budapest and its environs', contained new principles of urban development. The programme considered Budapest and its environs – the area of the later Greater Budapest – as a united metropolitan area. In order to relieve some of the burden on the capital, the plan promised an autonomous social and institutional life for the outlying settlements, as well as conditions for residential and working functions.

The idea of the north–south development of the capital was expressed here for the first time; this envisaged mainly residential and recreational functions along the northern course of the Danube, and industrial development towards the south. According to the plans, Buda was to be primarily a residential area, with the Pest side, the commercial and industrial centre.

The centralized city, which had developed around a single centre, was now envisaged as a decentralized one, broken up into a number of sub-centres. The troublesome industrial establishments were to be transferred to the southern and south-eastern parts of the city. It was at that time, too, that the idea of green areas of the city was expressed: green belts surrounding the inhabited areas and green strips penetrating the inner parts of the city. The increased involvement of public capital was also planned, on top of individual private construction.

These ideas were related to the most modern trends of international urbanistics, and to the planning and architecture that embraced the whole of contemporary Western Europe. It aimed not only at physical and technical planning, but also at the handling of social tensions in spatial terms. The avant-garde architecture of Western Europe, and the Soviet constructivism that flourished in the thirties, saw collective housing and housing estates as the solution to social and spatial tensions, and

142

especially to the housing problems of the working class. These ideas inspired some of the modern blocks of flats that were built in Budapest in that period. The first housing estates were built in the outlying working-class districts that had been neglected by earlier planning.

Centralized urban planning

After the Communist takeover in 1949, it became impossible to realize these earlier plans, and the processes that had been set in motion were abandoned. The Commission of Public Works was abolished; its sphere of authority was handed over to the newly-established Ministry of Building and Public Works. The Ministry, however, only had a formal decision-making right, as it was the Council of Ministers which took the decisions on the most diverse issues of urban development.

Central authority subordinated the processes of planning to its own ideological and economic interests. Urban development was interpreted as a sector of the national plan. Stress was laid on its subordinate role. The main objective of the state socialist authorities was accelerated industrial development, the establishment of heavy industry, and the development of an autonomous national economy – partly in preparation for a possible World War III, and partly for the ideological vision of spectacular economic growth. The idea was that this strained pace of development would bring Hungary up to the economic level of Western Europe. In the interests of a normative economic development that completely disregarded reality, agriculture was de-emphasized and its surplus income was poured into industrialization. At the same time many infrastructural investments, such as housing and the development of residential areas, were reduced to a minimum.

The state socialist political structure, and the centralized management of society, eliminated the possibility of local planning. Municipal authorities were stripped of all legal and financial means of planning. Funds were diverted away from communities and their development needs, and were redistributed according to the interests and preferences of the central authorities. From the 1960s redistribution took place behind the scenes, and was the product of informal bargaining within the plan. Local authorities had no say in these planning processes, and could not represent the inhabitants' housing or residency needs. Urban planning was no longer based even on a limited social consensus between the decision-makers and the inhabitants: the public conflicts of interest – between entrepreneurs, property owners, and tenants – had ceased. Decisions on issues of urban development were made within the internal bargaining processes of state institutions, independent of the inhabitants, socially interested groups, or the public.

Plans and planners

A consequence of the new processes was that urban development became dependent upon the central authorities. This meant that the ideas of planners repeatedly changed as the interests of those in power changed. But it also resulted in the planners developing their own sphere of interests. These new interests, however, favoured a group of urban planners who were different from their predecessors.

The logic of centralization dictated that, in the 1950s, urban planning moved from private design offices into state-controlled offices. These offices absorbed the best private planners and architects, but the power structure was different. The planners and architects who had been educated in modern West European schools, who had studied in Paris, London or Rome, were pushed into the background. This was particularly the case in the Ministry of Building, at the Municipal Council, and in district councils. The architects and planners who occupied the decision-making positions were those who had committed themselves to the so-called Soviet socialist realist architecture, and who had studied in the Soviet Union. This group acquired great power with the introduction of Soviet practices of planning in Hungary, and the introduction of so-called socialist urban planning, but particularly with the development of the new housing estates.

The consistent aim of the central authorities was to find some solution to the contradictions between economic policy and the ideology which promised a better and happier life than any previous political system, including housing for everybody. The solution was suggested by the large-scale development of housing estates.

The new housing schemes seemed suitable for the realization of all central objectives. They efficiently settled the labour required for rapid industrialization; they promised the fastest and thus the most spectacular development; they reduced the cost of infrastructure and housing to a minimum; and through the allocation of flats to the working class (the basis of state socialist power), the estates served the political and economic interests of the authorities. The ideas of leftist trends in urbanistics from the 1920s could also be utilized: that the housing estates offered the best conditions for community life.

Urban planners were given an unprecedented opportunity for interfering in the spatial structure of towns and cities. The opportunities for city planning had earlier been limited by the institutions of private property, by the restrictions due to the ownership of plots, and the preponderance of private development. The new possibilities were attractive for many architects. Interest in urban planning in Budapest was further promoted by the fact that the planners were given the opportunity of organizing large construction projects at a time when practically nothing was being built in other settlements, with the exception of the new industrial towns. The scale of development gave considerable power to the urban planners, for they were building the flats that had been long and eagerly awaited by many. Moreover, right until the late fifties it was the architects of the big design offices of the capital who directed the planning of country towns as well.

Changes in the centralization of city planning

The reform processes unfolding in the 1960s modified the features of city planning in a certain sense. In the sixties, and particularly in the seventies, some settlements, especially the county seats and larger towns, acquired greater economic strength. A government resolution of 1970 designated the favourably positioned and dynamically developing settlements and the large- and medium-sized towns as the foci of economic development. According to this resolution, factories with modern technology requiring highly qualified staff should be established in the regional centres. Through this concept of economic development, which embraced partial decentralization, some big towns acquired a political bargaining position which they were able to use to acquire larger funds for development and planning opportunities. The larger towns and county seats became autonomous centres of redistribution, and they themselves decided upon the spatial location and utilization of resources for infrastructural and housing development. The National Concept of the Development of the Settlement Network, an application of central place theory published in 1971, legitimized the situation that had evolved. It ranked settlements according to size and functions, classifying them in a hierarchical order. It also stated that the needs of production and of the population would be allocated according to the respective roles of settlements. This both confirmed and laid the basis for the unequal allocation of funds for settlement development. The county towns secured advantages mainly for themselves, and for the larger villages and towns, to the detriment of villages in a weaker bargaining position in the allocation of available resources. Consequently, the resources of development were utilized in the county centres and larger settlements, and regional and social inequalities were accentuated.

The changes that took place altered the conditions of centralized planning as well. Planning, while still organized within hierarchical relations, did not have a single centre any more, but developed a number of centres where planning was organized by bargaining processes that now bore evidence of reciprocity. This harmed those interests asserting the authority of Budapest, in so far as the capital was now obliged to share its power with the strengthened regional centres.

Table 9.1 shows that, until the 1960s, Budapest held the advantage in the national struggle for the distribution of resources for flat construction.

Table 9.1 Proportion of new flats built in housing estates, according to types of settlement (per cent)

Settlements	1959	1960–69	1970–79
Budapest	39.5	34.0	32.2
Towns	53.2	64.0	64.8
Of which:			
5 regional centres	9.3	17.3	22.2
New towns	21.5	13.8	7.5
Other towns	22.4	32.9	35.1
Villages	7.3	2.0	3.0
Total	100.0	100.0	100.0
N	63,141	123,954	333,543

Source: *A lakótelepek főbb adatai* (Main data on housing estates), Central Statistical Office, Budapest, 1983.

After 1960, and particularly after 1970, the five big towns which had gained significant strength received an ever-greater share of the available resources. During that period the proportion of new flats declined not only in the capital, but also in the new industrial towns. These resources were re-oriented to the five big towns and to other towns.

The struggle over redistribution was not only for new flats. The subsidized development of housing estates was naturally complemented by other kinds of institutions, such as crèches, kindergartens, schools and health centres. Very little state funding was earmarked for private flat development or related institutions outside the state sphere, and it was extremely difficult to gain access to it.

Physical plans

The history of physical plans is a good indicator of the changes that have taken place in centralized city planning, as well as of the conflicts of interest behind these changes and the power relations of the various regional interest groups.

After the abolition of the Commission of Public Works, the first new, general Master Plan of the capital was prepared by the Institute of Building Science and Design in 1948. However, it was not accepted by the government. A central resolution called upon the Mayor of Budapest to present his ideas for a long-term plan of the capital, confirmed by the National Planning Office and the Ministry of Building and Public Works, to the Council of Ministers, and to ask for a decision about the basic points of the city plan. The Municipal Council elaborated the new plan between 1951 and 1954; it was endorsed by the government only in 1960.

The Plan covered the capital as well as the sixty-four neighbouring settlements. The idea of north–south development had gone, and in its place the radial extension of the existing urban structure was recommended. The basic concept of the Plan was the restricted development of the territory of the capital, and the reduction in the number of inhabitants: it set the long-term plan at 2.3 million inhabitants, with another 550,000 people around the capital. The plans for housing and industrial development were unambiguously aimed at the restricted growth of the capital. In the sixties, far fewer flats were built in the capital than were needed or would have been justified by the proportion of the total population living in Budapest. In keeping with national ideas of decentralization, the settlement of new industries practically prohibited industrial development in the capital: new industrial estates were allowed only for servicing and storage, not only in the capital but also in its environs.

Besides the restricted development of Budapest, the Plan reckoned on the dynamic growth of neighbouring areas. It presented a picture of the densely-built-up territory of the city surrounded by a modern belt of communities, the urban centres of which, would be broken up by sparsely-built areas and industrial and green zones. The suburban settlements were supposed to safeguard the labour market of the capital with large dormitory communities of 5–6,000 flats and satellite towns, while they reduced commuting towards the capital and accommodated the migrant population coming in from the country.

In practice, little has been realized of the dormitory communities and satellite towns around the capital. This was not because planning was wrong about the expected regional social processes: the extent of in-migration did not cease even after the sixties. The idea of the satellite towns came to grief on the processes of informal bargaining, which underlay the changes in regional power relations.

It had already become clear by the time of the 1960 Master Plan that the countryside, unjustly pushed into the background in the fifties, was no longer prepared to accept an urban development focused on the capital and the new towns. The demand for the decentralization of public administration, planning and development were intensifying. In the early sixties Boudeville's well-known theory of growth poles was applied by the planners when the so-called concept of counter-poles was developed. This was the national settlement development aspect of economic reform that aimed at decentralization. The system of counter-poles served the reduction of the over-crowded and over-centralized capital by the development of eight regional planning units. Each region was supposed to develop on the basis of the co-operation of three or four counties. The centralization of the regional counter-poles was supposed to be counter-balanced by the development of a further 134 small towns as local centres. Some other plans were also elaborated for the differentiated development of certain regions, including the metropolitan area of Budapest. The 'Master Plan of the Metropolitan Area of Budapest' attempted to relieve the over-centralized capital by the development of an agglomeration, and a ring of towns and settlements surrounding it. The Plan proposed the development of eight large villages and small towns and their regions around the capital.

At the planning level there was no conflict of interest between the regional counter-pole and the region of Budapest, but a struggle ensued because of the shortage of resources. The theory of counter-poles had been carved up by the time it emerged victorious from the underlying struggle of informal interests for resources. The central planning authorities, partly because of the slow-down of decentralization, appointed only five counter-poles, the five largest county centres of Miskolc, Szeged, Pécs, Debrecen and Győr – to relieve the region of Budapest.

The concept of satellite towns had nothing to offer these regional centres, as the attraction of the new towns would have endangered the labour market of the latter. The capital was afraid that the outlying districts would develop into strong regions on its borders. Consequently, the development funds were separated: the money for the surrounding area was allocated to Pest county, to which it belonged so that Budapest could not interfere in its utilization. Even Budapest rejected the idea of satellite towns. The idea was fashionable at the time among western urban planners, but its Hungarian adaptation was challenged by a number of central planners in Hungary because of the high costs involved. Moreover, Budapest was interested in cheap labour. This is what the less developed areas on its borders could offer, so there was no need for expensive middle-class satellite towns. As a result, the masses of in-migrants arriving there were forced to start building their own homes under extremely adverse infrastructural and other conditions, but they had better accommodation than in the new housing estates.

Decentralization came to a halt during the 1960s, and the power of the capital to assert its interests started to grow again. The Master Plan of 1970 unambiguously rejected exaggerated views demanding the restriction of growth. It also rejected acceleration in favour of slow development. However, territorial growth was not allowed because of the expected cost of transport and public amenities, and instead it promoted stretches of development along existing lines of transport as the most economical and functional form of growth. According to the Plan, there was a possibility for parallel development of residential, industrial and green areas. The construction of a network of fast transport was decided upon in the interests of safeguarding development within corridors. The Plan permitted the growth of residential areas only in concentrated form, by the construction of housing estates. Territorial extension was to be avoided through greater building density in the inner parts of the city, and through reconstruction.

According to the settlement plan of 1970, the housing shortage was to be eliminated by 1985: the construction of 410,000 flats and the destruction of 150,000 was envisaged between 1970 and 2000. In the environs of the city, the construction of mainly detached family houses was to be encouraged. Under the plan, any territorial extension which became necessary would be most advantageous towards the north, along both sides of the Danube. The plans related to the building of industries also limited territorial increases. Only such industries were supposed to be developed which had already been established and could not be developed elsewhere, and where transport was available and opportunities existed for co-operation. The plan did not consider the establishment of new industries on the territory of the existing industrial belt around the city to be justified.

In practice, the 'realization of reconstruction work was postponed', and the construction of new settlements in the open spaces that were still available continued. Hence, the extensive development of the city was maintained. Extensive development of housing estates characterized growth in the agglomeration belt, as well as the building of detached houses.

The 1980 Master Plan of Budapest maintained the concept of a concentrated state housing programme, though the sale of new, so-called freehold flats, built by the state but intended for private ownership, was becoming increasingly difficult. The Plan proposed the development of the area parallel to the river because of the profitable conditions of transport and public amenities. About 47 per cent of the housing estates were planned for the north, and 29 per cent for the south, partly through the reconstruction of low-quality buildings, and partly through the utilization of vacant, mainly agricultural, land. Pesterzsébet, Újpest, Angyalföld, Kispest, Káposztásmegyer, Újpalota and Csepel were earmarked for this purpose. Thus, the residential areas of the city were to be extended further, to the extent that a continuous belt of housing estates has developed around the capital, housing almost half of the city population.

The number of flats built by the state dropped radically between 1981 and 1985 all over the country. The decrease was even greater after 1985. In 1987 and 1988 most construction still underway was completed in Budapest, and there remained hardly any building activity in the rest of the country outside the five large cities (see Table 9.2).

A high price had to be paid for this forcibly-maintained extensive urban development: the green spaces have further decreased. People turned to whatever solution they could find; the demand for privately-owned plots for second homes started to grow, and agricultural lands

149

Table 9.2 Proportion of new flats by type of settlement, 1981–1988

	1981–5		1986		1987		1988	
	State	Private	State	Private	State	Private	State	Private
Budapest	39.4	14.0	27.7	12.6	44.3	13.9	50.2	12.9
Other towns	52.0	41.4	59.6	46.6	46.6	45.1	39.0	45.1
Villages	8.6	44.6	12.7	40.8	9.1	41.0	10.8	42.0
Percentage	100.0	100.0	100.0	100.0	100.0	100.0	100.0	100.0
Total	81,483	288,201	7,622	61,806	7,769	49,431	5,209	45,357

Source: *A lakótelepek fő adatai* (Main data on housing estates), Central Statistical Office, Budapest, 1983.

were massively utilized for that purpose, despite the regulations. There were hardly any funds for the development of transport; only the route of the M0 motorway, the ring road round Budapest constituting the backbone of the road network, was marked out, and the path of the M4 was altered.

In keeping with the hierarchical logic of the national settlement planning and development of 1971, a hierarchical system of graded centres was developed in the capital. Although settlement development experts and sociologists challenged it, the concentrated utilization of economic resources was considered by the ideology that ruled in planning to be not only economically, but also socially effective. The infrastructure, developed around a central location, was supposed to be accessible for the population.

As conceived in the idea of a system of centres, the inner city of Budapest was to be not only the administrative centre of the capital, but also a national centre and the headquarters of Pest county, as well as playing a role in the supply of the agglomeration belt. A significant proportion of the institutions of commerce, culture and higher education was located there. In order to relieve the main centre, the Plan foresaw the development of six sub-centres for the parts of the city linked to the inner districts. These sub-centres were to be developed at Újpest in the north of the city, at Zugló in the east, at Kispest in the south, at Óbuda in the northern part of Buda, in the region between Moscow Square and the Southern railway station for the hilly area, and at Lágymányos for the south. The sub-centres would be basically developed from local functions, but would perform roles for the neighbourhood as well. And they would take over certain commercial and cultural functions of the main centre. As prescribed by the Plan, the intensity of building was to be reduced in the city centres in order to locate the necessary institutions there, and to develop the network of roads, car parks and pedestrian precincts. The significance of the traditional district centres, defined as having roles of medium importance, was to be retained as well. In the outer settlement belt, Szentendre, Dunakeszi, Szigetszentmiklós, Érd, Rákoskeresztúr, Kistarcsa, Vecsés, Pesthidegkút and Pilisvörösvár were to become the centres of groups of settlements.

The decisive factor in the planners' selection of the smallest possible number of centres and spheres of attraction was not so much social, as economic. The Plan stated that it was impossible to arrange central functions for all twenty-two districts and forty-five suburban settlements. It was acknowledged that it was the new housing estates which had forced the concept of sub-centres and the regional distribution of institutions concentrated in the capital. Therefore it was the new parts of the city and the capital's planning authorities which were mostly interested in the allocation of institutions to the new areas; the new sub-centres, developed along the existing infrastructure and transport links of the new housing estates, were the least expensive.

The hierarchical interpretation of the urban centres began to change in response to the demands for decentralization all over the country, and on account of the renewed reform processes of the 1980s. The Master Plan of 1980 mixed the levels of supply, although the central functions were still partially, if less rigidly, separated in spatial terms. Three earlier district centres were renamed as city centres. The spheres of attraction of Csepel, Pesterzsébet and Kőbánya have extended over the entire capital, with the exception of the inner areas, and even over the villages in the agglomeration belt. According to the surveys of 1980, commuting remained significant because of the housing and industrial policies of the agglomeration. Partly because of this, and partly because of the earlier infrastructural backwardness, the desired nine centres of the suburban zone could not develop. Therefore, the Plan earmarked only six centres. They were Szentendre, Dunakeszi, Kerepestarcsa, Rákoskeresztúr, Szigetszentmiklós and Érd.

The social legitimation of planning again came to the fore. The 1980 Plan criticized the fact that the number of urban sub-centres was set only on the basis of economic considerations, irrespective of social demands. Ultimately the number of urban sub-centres earmarked for development was reduced, in the capital as well as in its suburban zone. Centralized planning was forced to retreat, primarily because of diminishing funds. Social interests were only considered when they favoured the interests of planning.

Urban planning was coming up with ideas on a smaller scale because the financial resources were drying up. Few changes were planned for the 1980s. According to the Master Plan, the basic structure of the capital and the existing body of the city was to remain essentially unchanged; only minor, internal structural changes were envisaged. The development of railways and the network of local trains, the broadening of the main roads and the extension of their network, the building of new sections of the main highways, the development of the airport and the river ports did not alter the existing urban structure. The building of housing estates was to slow down after 1990 and be replaced by the reconstruction of the inner city. The outer districts of the capital were to become gradually more densely built-up; the quantity of buildings was to grow by 30 to 40 per cent. As a consequence of these processes, the different parts of the city were to become more urbanized, and the differences in standards was to be reduced between the inner and outer areas. With industrial growth limited in the capital, the industrial zones earmarked for development abundantly covered the demand, and significant tracts of land remained unused. According to the 1980 Plan, the territory earmarked for industrialization was sufficient, and the further development of industrial estates that did not disturb the environment was not restricted.

Budapest has not had a single settlement plan which was so short-lived as the Master Plan approved in 1988, even though this Plan was the most up-to-date in its decentralizing outlook, in its concept of intensive development and open planning. It proposed the decentralized institutional development of the city, it intended to increase the number of urban and district centres, and it wished to locate sports and health care institutions, requiring quiet, cleanliness and greenery, in the outer parts. The Plan wanted to remove polluting industrial activity into industrial zones prepared for that purpose, although only if it was possible to achieve 'removal without losses'. It stated that the centre of gravity of development was to be in the inner parts of the city, where emphasis was laid on rehabilitation, on the growth in the intensity of building, and on the effective protection of historical monuments and environmental elements. According to the basic concept of the Plan, the territorial structure of the capital and its environs would not fundamentally change until the turn of the century. Some territorial growth was envisaged by new individual and group housing. The stock of flats would be modified by two major processes: first, by the intensive transformation of the suburban belt of detached family houses and the building of private semi-detached houses, and secondly, by the rehabilitation of the inner city. The settlement plan expected a fall in population. Forecasts estimated that the number of inhabitants would decrease by about 80,000 within fifteen years. In the 1990 census the number of inhabitants of Budapest had fallen by almost 44,000 between 1980 and 1990.

The Master Plan outlined the development conception of the capital for fifteen years and outlined certain (mainly infrastructural) elements for thirty years. However, at the beginning of the 1990s the socio-political transition raised the question of whether a new plan was needed. There are a number of reasons for thinking that it is. The old plan did not take into consideration the hosting of the World Exhibition, or the appearance of the demands of entrepreneurial capital, including western capital. A change is needed basically because of the accelerated decentralization of planning, and because of the requirements of local plans. The 1990 Act LXV on local government, grants the opportunity of autonomous planning and development to the communities and urban districts, though the financial resources have not yet been clarified.

In the course of planning, no attention was paid to property ownership relations when asserting state interests, mainly because of the dominance of state ownership and because land and different kinds of property had no market value. New planning will be necessary after the transformation of ownership relations and the privatization of urban land. The growth in the significance of land owned by private individuals and by local governments would reshape the relationship between state and local authority planning, and in general the significance of planning by the authorities would be reduced, to the benefit of spontaneous market mechanisms. Nevertheless, the processes determining the transformation of planning have not come to an end: the realignment of interests is still continuing, and is particularly difficult in the capital. It has not yet been decided whether property such as flats and buildings will be handed over to private owners or to the local authorities. Or to what extent profit from the market economy serves the interests of the state, the local authorities or private owners. And there are other questions. What is the relationship between local authorities and the capital? What will happen to the districts, and to the different parts of the city? What are the criteria of decentralization? Will local authorities be interested in planning and development based on local integration? The questions that remain leave undecided what the regional role of the capital will be.

Planning and the handling of social tensions

The Master Plans indicate how approaches have changed, and how urban planning has become increasingly complex. From the seventies onwards, urban planning, which had previously been focused strongly around the architects, has been shaped by the co-operation of a growing number of professions and interests, including architects, transport experts, civil engineers, economists, landscape designers and social scientists. This process has become so advanced that, according to some, the architectural viewpoint has been pushed too far into the background.

A more complex approach to city planning, aimed at the integration of a number of professional interests, has had a number of results: the infrastructure of the city has been extended and modernized, and an up-to-date network of roads and public transport, railway stations, fast trams, buses and underground has been developed. This network links the new housing estates, the new parts of the city, the old suburban districts and settlements, to the districts and centres. The transport and road networks also maintain contact with the agglomeration. A modern system of public utilities in the capital has also been developed.

Changes in the interest-asserting power of the different professions participating in city planning are manifest in this new approach. Transport and water supply groups were able to assert their interests strongly in the seventies, whereas interest groups involved with the protection of the landscape, of the environment and of monuments has played an increasingly important role in the mid-eighties.

It has been shown that the planning of the previous century did not seek to handle territorial social tensions. Therefore a question remains as to what the relationship of state socialist planning was to social tensions and regional conflicts. The highly centralized planning of the fifties, which was cut off from social demand because of the power relations of the state and the lack of any market, could only play an ideologically manipulative role. It did not seek to settle social conflicts. Later on it was only able to represent and treat social interests which corresponded to the political and power interests because of its hierarchical limitations. One of its main tasks was ideologically to ensure its social legitimacy among those who had been left out.

The planning of the sixties was given realistic opportunities to represent territorial social interests, which was indispensable in terms of the functioning of the political system. This is how the situation remained until it turned out that the available resources were only sufficient to serve the objectives of the authorities in the running of the system. It was at that time that the legitimizing role of city planning came to the fore: contemporary documents speak about the levelling of social inequalities, despite their growth in the different regions.

The seventies were somewhat more open. But planning still contained the normative targets usually found in socialist city planning which contradicted the realistic objectives of the plan, the tasks it outlined and the processes of real life, for instance, such ideas as balanced development between the different settlements and parts of the city; the elimination of differences in the supply of population, or the principle of the proportionate development of sectors (such as housing, transport and the road network). The bare consideration of economics was in itself a legitimate one.

In the eighties there has been no possibility of, and no necessity for, the social legitimation of city planning. It has become obvious – partly due to scientific research – that the interests omitted from city planning have an articulated structure. In the wake of the political changes, the demand for social decentralization has become not only louder, but also more realistic. All of which renders unnecessary ideological legitimacy and the treatment of social tension omitted from the integrative mechanisms of hierarchical city planning. By the beginning of 1990, all conditions are in place for the development of urban planning which expresses the differentiated structure of, and openly confronts, the interests in a modern metropolitan society.

10
The administration of the city

The historical roots of centralized administration

The chapters above have made it clear that no real urban local government could function under the state socialist system, that citizens had no
chance of setting up organizations on their own initiative, and that the
intervention and control of the state (central government) was overwhelming. However, centralizing efforts date back not just to the
Communist takeover, or even to the establishment of nineteenth-century
modern public administration.

Medieval Hungarian towns had far less autonomy than Western European ones. The economic autonomy of western cities had appeared in the
early Middle Ages, and was a precondition of mercantile capitalism and
the development of capital accumulation. East Central European towns
had stronger feudal dependencies. In Hungary, towns in a better position
were the so-called 'royal free boroughs' (such as Pest and Buda), which
came under direct royal control, and had greater rights of jurisdiction
and self-government. During the first part of the sixteenth century, Buda
and Pest were occupied by the Ottoman Empire, and did not regain their
former rights after their liberation in 1686. The local authorities were
appointed from above, and the administration was headed by a Mayor
in Buda and a Justice in Pest, both Austrian imperial officials. But the
appointed local authority immediately launched a struggle for autonomy.
The local authority of Buda addressed a memorandum to the monarch
for the return of the urban privileges of pre-Turkish times. In 1703,
when the Treasury was in financial difficulty, Emperor Leopold I
declared Pest and Buda once more royal free boroughs, though only in
return for the payment of considerable sums. Consequently, the two

towns were again put directly under the authority of the Crown. They were exempted from feudal services (the payment of ninths to the landlord and tithes to the Church), were given the right to collect duties and mete out justice, and could elect some of their officials.

History has continued to follow the same pattern. In the late eighteenth century, centralization gained impetus; local government consisted of appointed officials of the state who were invested with full powers. In the early nineteenth century, local governmental rights were extended and the War of Liberation of 1848–9 created a real local government, which was again followed by vigorous centralization after the uprising was crushed. At first a military administration was introduced. Then, urban bodies of forty-two members in Pest and thirty members in Buda were appointed in 1851. Elections were held for the first time in 1860. This see-saw has operated ever since the introduction of modern public administration (1867). When the central government gets weaker, it yields to the local authorities, and whenever it regains its strength, its earlier position is restored. Budapest itself has a dual soul in this process: as a capital it draws certain benefits from centralization, and it can assert its interests better through central government than the country towns. In periods of centralization the state is all-pervasive; when local government is strong, various professional and social organizations have a greater role compared to the elected local authority. The alternating of concentration and diffusion of authority also occurs between the capital and district authorities.

The past 100 years or so can be divided into two major periods. The first period began with the 1872 Act XXXIV declaring the merger of Buda, Pest and Óbuda and its administration, and it lasted until 1950, with modifications introduced in the early 1920s. The second period was that of the system of councils between 1950 and 1990. The Local Government Act passed in the summer of 1990 has again opened a new period in the history of the government of the capital.

The administration of Budapest (1873–1950)

The Act on the Community passed one year before the merger distinguished three kinds of settlement administration: those of towns, large villages and small settlements (which were able to offer full administrative services only jointly, together with a number of small settlements or large villages). Later (1876), some towns were given administrative rights equivalent to those of the counties. Naturally, Budapest was given the right of a county. It had already become so prominent at the time of the introduction of modern public administration that its functioning was regulated by a separate Act.

Plans and planners

The rights of local government were exercised by the elected representative body of the capital in the regular plenary sessions. The general assembly had the right to determine the conditions of economic activities (including local taxes), to take loans, and to delineate the administrative districts and constituencies. The powers of the local authority also had significant limitations. For instance, considerable powers in the field of construction were wielded by the Commission of Public Works, which – as has been described above – was an organization located between the municipal body of representatives and the government. However, the greatest limitation was that the general assembly had to choose the chief mayor from three candidates nominated by the monarch; thus, the mayor was a representative of the government. The municipal police – largely financed by the capital – was also under the control of the government. Although there were repeated efforts to make a new bill on the capital, the divided general assembly could not agree upon its content.

The 1872 Act spelt out who were the main officials of the capital. They were the chief mayor, the mayor, the deputy mayors, the councillors, the chief notary, the notaries of the council, the district notaries, the chief prosecutor, the prosecutors, the chief medical officer, the district medical officers, the chief auditor and the chief archivist. The officials were elected by the representatives for a period of seven years.

The districts of the capital had very limited autonomy. They were subordinate to the municipal body of representatives. There were four to eight elected jurors, beside the district chief, who were paid non-professional citizens rather than full-time staff. The 1893 Act on the district magistracy granted the districts powers similar to those of the autonomous settlements, but the head and members of magistracy were elected by the municipal body of representatives, and the population could no longer elect their representatives into the bodies governing the districts. A significant professional apparatus was developed in the districts and functioned as the first tier of authority. The expanding and modernizing administrative organization of the capital concentrated upon the development of the infrastructure, on urban policy, and on the handling of social tensions that came with metropolitan growth. In the first decade of the twentieth century, the capital implemented major investments in social housing and the building of schools and cultural institutions.

At the turn of the century the city's most important property was its land and buildings. The overwhelming majority of financial income derived from taxes. The capital levied additional taxes even on state taxes; local taxes were introduced, and duties were collected upon certain products brought to the capital. However, income from taxation was becoming increasingly inadequate to cover the growing costs of building a modern city. The majority of in-migrants that swelled the population were weak taxpayers. The capital took on large loans and was heavily in debt by the first part of the twentieth century. The city set up a series of lucrative public service enterprises such as an urban transport company, gas and electrical power stations, an advertisement company, and even a bakery and food store network. Community enterprises had gained great significance by the end of the nineteenth century in the economy of the city.

The 1872 law on the capital, since which the city's administration system has been regulated by separate law, guaranteed the presence of the largest taxpayers in urban representative bodies. Suffrage was limited; conditions of wealth, schooling and local residence excluded a large part of the citizenry from asserting their interests in urban policy. Half of the members of the representative body consisted of the largest taxpayers, so that only one half was elected. Until the 1890s, 3 per cent, and even in the 1910s, 5 per cent of the total population was entitled to vote. Decisions were taken by rich citizens on urban policy which favoured large-scale building activities and the promotion of the economy, but increased social tensions as well. From the end of the nineteenth century, liberal intellectuals increasingly demanded the introduction of universal adult suffrage and the abolition of the privileges of the large taxpayers. This was ultimately achieved in 1917, during World War I, when radical political movements gained strength in the country. It was at this time that the King permitted the municipal general assembly to introduce a universal, equal and secret franchise in the election of the capital's representative body. It should also be noted that industrial capitalism had by then been generally strengthened, and administrative means were no longer needed for its support.

The principles and organization of the government of the capital changed little during the inter-war period. The number of voters increased to 30 per cent of the population. The internal territorial division of the city changed with the expansion of the population and the built-up area (in 1872 the capital was divided into ten, and in 1930, into fourteen districts), and the plan for a 'Greater Budapest' (the administrative union of the peripheral settlements with the capital) took shape and was ultimately accomplished in 1950.

In October 1945 after the end of World War II, local elections were held; the mandate of the then elected representative body expired in 1948, but it was extended until the end of 1949, when this period of local government drew to a close. In 1949 the country passed a socialist constitution (which was not so much an adaptation as a translation of the Soviet constitution), and the system of councils was introduced in 1950.

Plans and planners

The system of councils (1950–90)

The establishment of councils was governed by Act I of 1950. The councils were the representatives of uniform state authority in the region under their power. The system of councils was an organization of public administration that differed in its basic principles from local government. Local councils were set up in each community, and the traditional system of counties and the special administrative status of the capital were retained. 'Involving the masses in the administration of their own affairs' was an important task of the councils; therefore, they had a relatively high number of members, with the different occupational groups, national minorities, age and gender groups and so forth enjoying proportionate representation. Besides the specialized agencies of the councils, a number of professional committees operated. The principle of 'socialist democracy' was to mobilize the masses, and to safeguard the primacy of overall social interests (that is, state control) against the local ones.

After forty years of the council system, certain features can be noted:

– Its introduction was a major break with the traditions of Hungarian public administration (which represented a European tradition). The adapted Soviet model was so incapable of operation that as early as 1954 a new Act on councils was passed which increased the autonomy of the local councils, and their direct subordination to central government was partially replaced by subordination to the county councils. The third Act on councils passed in 1971 departed even further from the original Soviet model in so far as the representation of the electorate and local government were included with the administrative functions as basic tasks of the councils. However, the councils did not become real local authorities, partly because of their financial dependence upon central government, and partly because the real foci of decision-making were the local (regional) party organizations (which exercised their authority mainly by informal methods in Hungary). Nevertheless, the modifications after 1971 preserved the strength of the European traditions of public administration, and their partial restoration prepared the ground for a shift to administration by local government.
– Although the members of the councils were re-elected every four years, the elections were not real ones. Voters had to choose between a list of candidates compiled by the Patriotic People's Front and approved by the party organizations. The members of the councils depended not on the electorate, but upon the organizations nominating them. From the 1970s onwards, multiple candidacy was permitted, though rarely applied. A major change occurred in the local elections of 1985 when multiple candidacy was made

obligatory, and nominations had to be made in open election meetings. To the party's great surprise, huge masses attended these meetings. Nominations could still be manipulated, yet about 30 per cent of the representatives on the local councils were not official nominees.

– The councils were 'responsible' for their community – not only for its public administration, but also for sports and cultural life: for example, they controlled the operation of the Churches, etc. Societies, associations and organizations which private individuals had set up were not permitted to operate in the local community, even though these had played such an important role in pre-war local governments. The different companies and offices had acquired great significance, and the scene of political socialization was shifted from the local communities to the workplace. In addition, the industrial enterprises and the agricultural co-operatives in the countryside had undertaken different socio-political and cultural functions.

The municipal council had a dual function: it performed both the tasks of the local council for the entire capital, and the functions of a county council by the control and co-ordination of the district councils (which operated as autonomous local councils). The sessions where the council took its decisions were for a long time formal affairs. The council met only four times a year, and usually passed the submitted proposals after a brief debate. The real power lay with the executive committee which met frequently, both because this body prepared the proposals that were to be discussed by the council session, and because the implementation of the decisions was in its hands. The executive committee was doubly subordinate: to the council which had elected its members, and to the Council of Ministers.

The administrative apparatus of the council was in the hands of the secretary of the executive committee. The post of secretary was an administrative job to which the holder was appointed; the chairman of the council (and his deputies) had a political function. The chairman presided over the sessions of both the council and the executive committee. The council operated specialist committees as well, the task of which was to control, propose and review, but primarily to participate in the different development programmes. The administrative apparatus, which answered to the executive committee, was made up of specialist agencies (such as the departments of public education, health, etc.). These organs controlled a number of institutions, including schools and hospitals. But here too there was double subordination: the specialist agencies were directed by the executive committee of the council as well as by the respective ministries (in other words the Ministries of Education and Health), which exercised professional control over them. The district

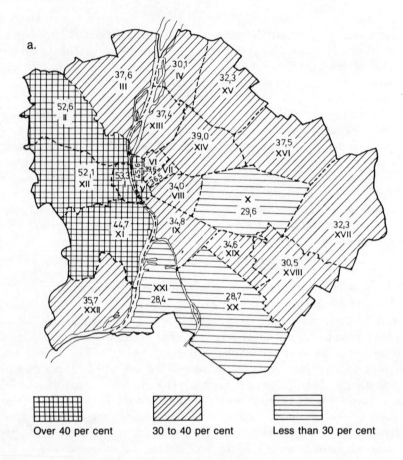

Over 40 per cent   30 to 40 per cent   Less than 30 per cent

Figure 10.1 Results of the 1990 municipal elections
a. Participation rate (per cent of the eligible population)

councils of the capital offered the basic services, but in some cases much more than that (for instance, they ran secondary schools).

The finances of the council were rigorously controlled by the government. The municipal council had considerable income from various sources, mainly from the contributions of council enterprises and from community taxes on the companies operating in the city. But half of the budget came from state grants. These grants were distributed among the district councils by the municipal council. Funds were earmarked for development, and for such compulsory expenses as the maintenance of public institutions, roads, etc. The economic reform introduced in 1968 did not extend to councils' economic management. The rigorous control

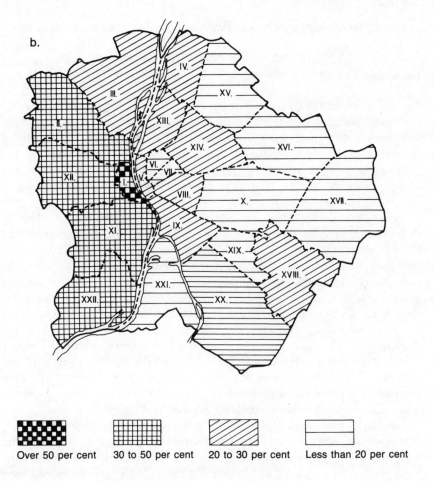

b.

Over 50 per cent   30 to 50 per cent   20 to 30 per cent   Less than 20 per cent

b. Percentage of votes for the government coalition (Hungarian Democratic Forum, Smallholders Party, Christian Democratic Party)

of finances and complex dependencies did not allow any sizeable local governmental economic activities.

In 1986, significant changes were introduced into economic management. The most important changes were that the councils were not tied in their use of the financial resources at their command, and that grants from the budget became normative. Earlier councils and towns had to engage in political bargaining over their share of the available grants from the state budget; of course, the capital had an advantage in this bargaining. In 1988, income tax was introduced, a part of which (it varied annually how much, and from 1990 covered the whole amount) was handed to the local councils. The growing financial autonomy of the

163

councils marked the transition towards a local government economy.

Local government administration

Parliament passed the Local Government Act on 3 August 1990. The Act had great political significance: after the free, multi-party elections held in March 1990, local authorities were also freely elected in autumn of the same year. This completed the democratization of the Hungarian political system. As a result, Hungary became a member of the Council of Europe at the end of 1990, the first country from among the former socialist countries.

Under the Act, Budapest has a two-tier public administration. The 22 districts represent as many local authorities which are not subordinated to the municipal general assembly. 25- to 40-member representative bodies are elected in the 22 districts, depending upon the number of inhabitants, and these bodies elect the district mayor. The municipal general assembly has 88 members: 66 are elected from party lists (voters elect both district and municipal representatives), and 22 members are delegated by the 22 districts. The municipal general assembly elects the chief mayor. The right-of-centre governmental coalition suffered a major defeat at the municipal elections, and acquired the mayorship in only one district. The left-of-centre liberal opposition (the Alliance of Free Democrats and of the federation of Young Democrats) was victorious. The chief mayor is also a member of the AFD.

The opposition municipal local authority is not going to be in an easy situation. It will be difficult to achieve co-operation between the autonomous district local authorities and the capital. It is not yet known how much state property will be handed to the local authorities and how it will be shared between the capital and the districts. The Local Government Act only ruled that a separate act is to be passed on the capital by 30 November 1990, but the relevant bill was not submitted to Parliament in 1990. An act was passed on local taxes: local authorities may levy separate taxes on real property and on industrial activity (and they are bound to levy those taxes because of budgetary constraints), which may bring about their unpopularity at the very beginning of their existence amidst rapidly falling living standards.

The rebirth of local government has launched political movements that are not advantageous from the point of view of expert public administration. After forty years of management from above, there is a strong desire for autonomy in every community and a strong suspicion of any 'superior authority' or hierarchy. The desire for independence has been very strong in the districts; moreover, attempts were even made for the establishment of partial local authorities within some districts (as is allowed by the Act). No reference has been made to co-operation within the Budapest agglomeration. Therefore, the beginnings of local government will – inevitably – be quite confused, until the authorities themselves become ready for regional (or intra-municipal) co-operation.

11
Conclusion: Budapest at the turn of the century

The moment is not that far away. Less than ten years and the world again reaches the turn of a century. Curiously enough, the turns of centuries have been particularly important for Budapest. We have seen that the city lived through one of the most spectacular and dynamic periods of its history at the turn of the twentieth century. This period was symbolized by the grandiose celebrations held in Budapest to mark the millennium of the country in 1896. It was then that the newly-erected buildings, public institutions, and museums were inaugurated, and new roads were opened. This display ended a long period of conflicting interests, when the Austrian empire and the Hungarian ruling circles had reached an agreement upon Hungarian bourgeois development within the framework of the Austrian empire, while the traits of a feudal structure, favouring the interests of the ruling groups and the privileges of the feudal aristocracy, were retained. The exhibition held in May 1896 was an exhibition of the victors. The middle classes, albeit to a lesser extent, also participated in the euphoria sweeping the country. The Compromise extended them protection against the increasingly radical *petit bourgeoisie* and the growing numbers of the working class. Urban development suited their interests as well. The excluded *petit bourgeois* masses and the workers did not share either the euphoria or the benefits of urban development.

Budapest is preparing to hold a World Fair prior to the turn of the twenty-first century. Are there factors that suggest an analogy? In 1896 Budapest and the forces desirous of embourgeoisement and independence wanted to show Vienna, and the world, that Budapest was the second capital of the Austro-Hungarian monarchy and a worthy rival to Vienna. A desire to present itself to the world could be found in 1987 as well, when the government decided upon the holding of the Vienna–Budapest World Fair with the support of various power groups, and more generally of those well informed about this issue. The decision indicated disagreement with the division of Europe in Yalta, and showed that the country wanted to join the Western World. This time Budapest did not want to compete with Vienna, but to make an alliance with it. The decision on the World Fair was a wish to symbolize the efforts towards the transformation of the economic system. The chance to realize the exhibition was based on a future economic model.

However, at the end of 1990, when after much wrangling the government commissioner for the World Fair went to Paris to register an application to organize the World Fair at the Bureau International des Expositions, the situation had completely changed. There was no agreement upon the issue even within the government, and no decision had been taken on the World Fair.

The political transformation has been accomplished, so the strenuous efforts that would accompany the World Fair are not required anymore, and Hungary does not have to show the world that it wants to get out of the Eastern bloc. It has got out of it, not least because the Eastern bloc has disintegrated. The demand for an economic transformation should be realized rather than displayed. In this sense the conditions for the World Fair have disappeared. However, there is another at least as important factor which delays, if not challenges, the issue of the Fair: the lack of a national compromise at the end of the twentieth, and the beginning of the twenty-first centuries. On the domestic political scene there is no historical moment resembling that of 1896, there are no winners and losers so far. In this sense the conditions for a World Fair are lacking.* There is not the euphoria, the sense of an era coming to an end, nor a social consensus involving a narrower or broader social circle. The bargaining that began over the dismantling of the state socialist structure in the early 1980s, which will determine the social, economic, political and regional development of the country and capital into the twenty-first century, has not been settled. At present, it is unknown what role Hungary and her territorial centre will play on the international stage. Subordination to the Soviet Union has come to an end, but its new dependencies and particularly its opportunities for autonomy have not been set. Nor has any international compromise for the twenty-first century been reached yet. It is not yet known what the turn of the century will bring: new and dynamic development, a new era of promise,

* During 1991 public opinion became more favourable towards the World Fair, and it was definitively accepted by the Bureau International des Expositions in February 1992.

achievements in the development of urban space and society, or crises and stubborn conflicts, which will still be awaiting a solution in the new century.

Theoretically, both alternatives are possible. The changes at the end of the twentieth century, such as the political and social transition, the development of democracy, the unfolding of a market economy, and a closer relationship with Western Europe all promise an age of prosperity for Budapest and for Hungary as a whole. The transformations that have taken place in Eastern Europe have given Budapest the chance of once again becoming the centre of Central Europe, a regional centre of the economic life, trade, politics, science, and arts of the region in the twenty-first century.

The nineteenth century showed that the future of Budapest depended on the changes in domestic power relations, on the processes of bargaining among the dominant groups, and on consensus. The struggle for power, both formal and informal, began several years ago between Budapest and the country, the capital and the major country towns. The countryside does not accept the prominent role of Budapest. Inequalities that have been produced by historical processes have not been accepted, and neither have the spatial inequalities resulting from state socialist territorial distribution. This is proven by, among other things, the opposition of the countryside to the World Fair: people in the country are afraid of the increase in inequalities between the different regions of the country and the capital because of the World Fair. Nor do people living in the countryside accept the hypothesis that if the development of the capital is under democratic parliamentary control, and market mechanisms safeguard the development of local governments, then a strong capital may be a real attraction and there may be an opportunity for co-operation on an equal footing for the rest of the country.

Territorial inequalities exist within the capital too. They could be found in different spheres during the past century, and in still others during the period of state socialism. Nineteenth-century capital favoured the inner parts of the city, which were required by the capitalist interests of the groups playing a central economic and political role. The outer zone of the capital had little access to development opportunities. State socialism preferred the peripheral zones under the aegis of working-class ideology, as a consequence of its own economic, political interests and those of planning. But this was so also because state socialism could not avoid the general rules of urbanization, as a result of which decentralization to varying degrees has replaced the urban explosion and the centralizing processes of economic and social forces everywhere in Europe.

State socialist authority tried to suppress the most diverse spatial social problems for a long time. And even if the deviant phenomena of crime, alcoholism, the growing number of suicides observed in peripheral social groups in slum areas of the city were mentioned, they were interpreted by the authorities as moral and mainly transitory phenomena. In fact, they were social problems typical of the first periods of metropolitan development; tensions were conditioned by ecological causes and macro-social transformations. Moreover, the political institutions of conflict management and the assertion of interests were missing, as were the means of urban planning.

But some changes had occurred by the 1980s: movements asserting particular local interests, and struggles for better housing and cleaner air got wider publicity. However, the state and the system of dependency organized from above, and the lack of autonomy in local government, ensured that these local alliances had little chance.

The relationships of residence were surrounded by a mystification in the official assessments and ideologies. The transformation of the relationships characteristic of modern urban societies was falsely interpreted, and the direction of future change was treated in a utopian way. It was not acknowledged that the dissolution and transformation of traditional human ties, and of family and neighbourhood relationships, are a natural corollary of urban development, and that real spatial community relations could not develop because of both the lack of an institutional system during socialist development, and the conflicting social interests that exist in large cities.

Nevertheless, one of the bases upon which the modern system of social relations has been organized in Budapest is segregation, although this segregation differs slightly from experience in other European cities. In Budapest the segregation of the wealthier social groups is more characteristic than that of poorer groups of lower social status. Curiously enough this social trend could be observed, not only under state socialism, but also in the period after the Compromise in the last century.

Today it is difficult to say what new spatial processes and changes can be expected in the twenty-first century, or what changes may occur in urban society, even if we analyse the long-term developmental trends. There are many unknowns: where the growing middle and *grand bourgeois* layers will prefer to live in the wake of bourgeois development; where they are likely to, or be ready to, invest; how this will fit in with the plans of the local authorities; whether they will choose to restore the inner parts of the city, or will live in the suburban zones closely attached to the main body of the city, conforming to the policies of the local authorities on land and taxation. It is also possible that the interests and status of both parts of the city will be strengthened, or that the inner zone and the old parts linked to it will be revalued, while the status of the agglomeration, the outer belt of housing estates and the suburbs, will deteriorate further with the resettlement of unskilled workers presently living in the decayed inner parts and in the low-prestige new housing estates who cannot afford the cost either of rehabilitation, or of housing in the new parts of the city. Nor is it certain how many people will be included in the group forced out by the dynamism of urban development: will only unskilled and uneducated workers be forced to move and give up their flats in the new housing estates, or will low-paid white-collar workers also be affected? Today there is no answer even to the question of what the situation of the social groups which have to leave the inner areas will be, and how they will respond – with resignation or with a struggle.

The future of Budapest – the answers to the questions raised and to those not yet formulated – basically depends on whether the city will be capable of preparing itself for the role of an international centre in the Central European region. The city possesses the possibilities needed for that role. The opportunity is not only due to the fact that it is the natural geographical centre of the region, and that it has the ability to act as a bridge linking West European, Balkan and Russian markets by the activation of trade and banking. There is no city other than Budapest in the Central European region which possesses the extensive infrastructure and transport facilities indispensable to the performance of the role of a centre.

Tourists are attracted by the geographical location, natural environment, hot and medicinal spas, hotels, and architectural masterpieces bearing the influence of Western as well as Eastern European culture, but also drawing from Hungarian roots. However, there are certain preconditions that must be satisfied. First of all, adequate legal safeguards offering security to domestic and international capital and enterprise should be created soon. Political life should become balanced, the state government and the local government of Budapest co-operating as parties on an equal footing, and they should jointly find a solution to the ecological challenges threatening the future of the city and the life of the people. It is important to ensure that the rehabilitation of the old buildings and areas of the city is not limited to isolated sections, but that there should be a positive conservation programme covering the entire city. The city authorities should not, for the sake of short-term economic interests, sacrifice the existing values of the city: an urban development of almost two millennia, which may not be as glamorous as some metropolises, but has an atmosphere and excitement unique to Budapest.

Bibliography

Aczél, G., Hidas, P., 1980, Újabb téveszmék? Vitairat Budapest fejlesztéséről (Further misconceptions? A pamphlet on the development of Budapest), *Urbanisztika*, Vol. 1, 4–7.

Andorka, R., 1982, *A társadalmi mobilitás változásai Magyarországon* (Changes in social mobility in Hungary), Gondolat Könyvkiadó, Budapest.

Bácskai, V., 1971, *Források Buda, Pest és Óbuda történethez. 1696–1873* (Sources on the history of Buda, Pest and Óbuda. 1696–1873), Published sources of the archives of Budapest, No. 1, Budapest.

Bácskai, V., 1989, *A vállalkozók előfutárai. Nagykereskedők a reformkori Pesten* (The forerunners of entrepreneurs. Wholesale traders in Pest of the reform period), Magvető Könyvkiadó, Budapest.

Barta, B., Vukovich, Gy., 1983, A lakáshelyzet alakulása s jellemzői (The changes and characteristics of the housing situation), *Lakáspolitikánkról*, 204–21, Kossuth Könyvkiadó, Budapest.

Bencze, I., Tajti, E., 1972, *Budapest, an industrial geographical approach* (translated by Compton, P. A.), Akadémiai Kiadó, Budapest.

Bene, L., 1928, *Budapest székesfőváros iparosai* (Craftsmen of the capital city of Budapest), Mimeo, Budapest.

Bene, L., 1945, *Nagy-Budapest tervének kialakulása* (The evolution of the plan of Greater Budapest), Mimeo, Budapest.

Berend, T. I., 1979, *A szocialista gazdaság fejlődése Magyarországon 1945–1975* (The development of socialist economy in Hungary 1945–1975), Kossuth Könyvkiadó, Budapest.

Berend, T. I., Ránki, Gy., 1961, A Budapest környéki ipari övezet kialakulásának és fejlődésének kérdéséhez (On the issue of the evolution and development of the industrial zone around Budapest), *Papers on the past of Budapest*, Vol. 14, 535–73, Akadémiai Kiadó, Budapest.

Berend, T. I., Ránki, Gy., 1975, *Economic development in East Central Europe in the 19th and 20th centuries*, Columbia University Press, New York.

Berkovics, Gy., 1976, *Világváros határában* (On the outskirts of a metropolis), Szépirodalmi Könyvkiadó, Budapest.

Bernát, T., Viszkei, M. (eds.), 1972, *Budapest társadalmának és gazdaságának száz éve*

Bibliography

(One hundred years of the society and economy of Budapest), Közgazdasági és Jogi Könyvkiadó, Budapest.

Bernát, T. (ed.), 1985, *An economic geography of Hungary*, Akadémiai Kiadó, Budapest.

Beynon, E. D., 1943, Budapest. An ecological study, *Geographical Review*, Vol. 3, 255-75.

Bora, Gy., 1979, The stages of development of the industrial system of Budapest, Hamilton, F. E. I., Kortus, B. (eds.), *The spatial structure of industrial systems*, PWN, Warszawa, 41-59.

Biczó, T., 1979, *Budapest egykor és ma* (Budapest past and present), Panoráma, Budapest.

Bierbauer, V., 1920, *A régi Buda-Pest építészete* (Architecture of the Old Buda and Pest), Pfeifer, Budapest.

Bierbauer, V., 1937, *A magyar építészet története* (History of Hungarian architecture), Révai Nyomda, Budapest.

Boldizsár, I., 1935, Egy pesti bérház szociográfiája (Sociography of a block of flats in Pest), *Magyar Kultúra*, Vol. XXII., Nos. 13-14, 101-7.

Borsos, B., Sodor, A., Zádor, M., 1959, *Budapest építészet története, városképei és emlékei* (The history of architecture of Budapest, the views and monuments of the city), Műszaki Könyvkiadó, Budapest.

Budapest és környéke általános rendezési terve (Master Plan of Budapest and its vicinity), 1960, The Municipal Council of Budapest, Budapest.

Budapest és környéke általános rendezési tervnek felülvizsgálata (The revision of the Master Plan of Budapest and its vicinity), 1969, The Municipal Council of Budapest, Budapest.

Budapest és környéke általános rendezési terve (The Master Plan of Budapest and its vicinity), 1970, The Municipal Council of Budapest, Budapest.

Budapest agglomeráció általános rendezési terve – városépítési koncepció (The Master Plan of the Budapest agglomeration – the concept of urban construction), 1980, The Municipal Council of Budapest, Budapest.

Budapest általános rendezési terve (The Master Plan of Budapest), 1988, The Municipal Council of Budapest, Budapest.

Budapest hosszútávú környezetvédelmi koncepciója (The long-term conception of environmental protection in Budapest), 1984, Budapesti Városépítési Tervező Vállalat, Budapest.

Bulla, M. (ed.), 1989, *Tanulmányok a hazánk környezeti állapota c. dokumentumhoz* (Papers on the document entitled the environmental condition of our country), Ministry of Environmental Protection and Water Management, Budapest.

Compton, A. P., 1979, Planning and spatial change in Budapest, Chapter 16, French, R. A., Hamilton, F. E. I., *The socialist city. Spatial structure and urban policy*, 461-92, John Wiley and Sons, New York.

Csanádi, G., Ladányi, J., 1987, *Budapest – a városszerkezet történetének és a különböző társadalmi csoportok városszerkezeti elhelyezkedésének vizsgálata* (Budapest – the study of the history of urban structure and the location of different social groups within it), No. 4, Department of Sociology, University of Economics, Budapest.

Csanádi, G., Ladányi, J., 1988, Társadalmi csoportok térbeni elkülönülésének különböző léptékekben történő vizsgálata Budapesten (The study of the spatial segregation of social groups of various scales in Budapest), *Szociológia*, Vol. 17, No. 1, 1-17.

Cséfalvay, Z., Pomázi, I., 1990, Az irányított dzsentrifikció egy budapesti program példáján (Controlled gentrification as exemplified by a Budapest programme), *Human Geographical Studies*, Vol. 51, No. 9, 27-39.

Csőregh, E., 1978, *A lakótelepi iskolások* (School children of housing estates), Akadémiai Kiadó, Budapest.

Dávid, G. J., 1983, A magánlakás-építés forrásai s feltételei (The sources and conditions of private housing), *Lakáspolitikánkról*, 150-75, Kossuth Könyvkiadó, Budapest.

Bibliography

Dienes, L., 1973, The Budapest agglomeration and Hungarian industry – a spatial dilemma, *Geographical Review*, 356–77.

Droste, W., 1988, *Budapest*, Ellert et Richter, Hamburg.

Dümmerth, D., 1968, *Pest város társadalma 1686–1696. A török hódoltság utáni első évtized lakosságának gazdasági, társadalmi és személyes életviszonyai Mária Terézia koráig* (The society of the city of Pest in 1686–1696. The economic, social and personal living conditions of the inhabitants during the first decade after the Turkish occupation until the age of Maria Theresa), Akadémiai Kiadó, Budapest.

Ekler, D., Hegedüs, J., Tomsics, I., 1980, *A városépítés alkalmazott társadalmi-gazdasági modelljének elméletei s módszertani kérdései* (Theoretical and methodological issues of the applied socio-economic model of city building), Budapesti Városépítési Tervező Vállalat, Budapest.

Enyedi, Gy., 1977, *Hungary. An Economic Geography*, Boulder, Westview.

Enyedi, Gy., 1978, The process of suburban development in Budapest, Enyedi, Gy., Mészáros, J. (eds.), *Urban Development in the USA and Hungary*, 137–47, Akadémiai Kiadó, Budapest.

Fodor, L., Illés, I., 1968, *Some problems of metropolitan industrial agglomeration*, Tempo Sokszorosító, Budapest.

Fodor, L., Schultz, J., 1972, *Budapest, Les grandes villes du monde*, Notes et Etudes Documentaires, La documentation française, No. 3886–7, La Documentation Française, Paris.

Fodor, L., 1973, *Falvak a nagyváros árnyékában* (Villages in the shadow of a metropolis), Kossuth Könyvkiadó, Budapest.

Fodor, L., 1978, Growth model of the Budapest agglomeration, Enyedi, Gy., Mészáros, J. (eds), *Urban development in the USA and Hungary*, 131–6, Akadémiai Kiadó, Budapest.

Fővárosi Közmunkák Tanácsa, 1893, *Építésügyi szabályzat Budapest fő- és székesfőváros területére* (Building regulations for the territory of the capital and royal seat of Budapest), Budapest.

Fővárosi Közmunkák Tanácsa, 1914, *Építésügyi szabályzat Budapest fő- és székesfőváros területére* (Building regulations for the territory of the capital city of Budapest), Budapest.

Fővárosi Közmunkák Tanácsa, 1940, *Építésügyi szabályzat Budapest fő- és székesfőváros területére* (Building regulations for the territory of the capital city of Budapest), Budapest.

Gárdonyi, A., 1910, *Budapest legrégibb kiváltságlevele* (The oldest patent of Budapest), Turul, booklets 2 and 3, Budapest.

Gábor, R. I., Galasi, P., 1979, A 'második gazdaság' módosító szerepe a társadalom szerkezetében (The modifying role of the 'second economy' in the social structure), *Társadalmi struktúránk fejlődése* (The development of our social structure), Vol. III, 145–79, Társadalomtudományi Intézet, Budapest.

Gáll, I., 1984, *A budapesti Duna-hidak* (The bridges over the Danube in Budapest), Műszaki Könyvkiadó, Budapest.

Gerő, L., 1973, *Pest-Buda építészete az egyesítéskor* (Architecture of Pest and Buda at the time of the merger), Műszaki Könyvkiadó, Budapest.

Granasztói, P., 1948, Nagy-Budapest városrendezése (Urban settlement of Greater-Budapest), *Városi Szemle*, Vol. 14, No. 1, 14–53.

Granasztói, P., 1966, Budapest városépítészeti arcképe (Images of Budapest in urban architecture), *Az építészet igézetében* (Under the spell of architecture), 117–47, Magvető Könyvkiadó, Budapest.

Granasztói, P., 1972, *Budapest vue par un architecte*, Corvina Könyvkiadó, Budapest.

Granasztói, P., 1974, Budapest arculatai (Faces of Budapest), *Az idő és a művek* (Time and Works), 147–253, Magvető Könyvkiadó, Budapest.

Hajdu, Z., 1989, Az 1956-os területbeosztási reformterv (The reform plan of territorial division for 1956), *Tér és társadalom*, Vol. 3, No. 4, 43–63.

Bibliography

Halandósági vizsgálatok. 2. A budapesti halandósági különbségek ökológiai vizsgálata 1980–1983 (Mortality surveys. 2. The ecological study of the differences of mortality in Budapest 1980–1983), Part I, 1986, Central Statistical Office, Budapest.

Haltenberger, M., 1943, *Budapest városföldrajzi képe* (The urban geographic image of Budapest), Idegenforgalmi Kiadó, Budapest.

Haltenberger, M., 1945, *Budapest elővárosai* (Suburbs of Budapest), Separate of Vol. XXX of the Városi Szemle, Budapest Székesfőváros Házinyomda, Budapest.

Harrer, F., 1940, *Budapest városfejlesztési programja* (Urban development programme of Budapest), Budapest Székesfőváros Házinyomda, Budapest.

Harrer, F., 1941, *A Fővárosi Közmunkák Tanácsa 1930–1940* (The Committee of Public Works of the capital, 1930–1940), Budapest.

Hegedüs, A., 1937, *Hungarian background*, III, Hamilton, London.

Hegedüs, J., Tosics, I., 1983, Lakáspolitika és lakáspiac (Housing policy and housing market), *Lakáspolitikánkról*, 261–96, Kossuth Könyvkiadó, Budapest.

Hegedüs, J., Tosics, I., 1983, Housing classes and housing policy: some changes in the Budapest housing market, *International Journal of Urban and Regional Research*, Vol. 7, No. 4, 467–94.

Helyzetkép a budapesti agglomercióról, 1980 (State of the Budapest agglomeration in 1980), Mimeo, 1981, Statisztikai Kiadó, Budapest.

Herskó, I., 1937, Budapest Székesfőváros kereskedő társadalma s annak helyzete (The merchant society and its situation of the capital city of Budapest), *Városi Szemle*, Vol. XXIII, No. 6, 907–19.

Hoffman, I., 1981, *Lakáskörülmények* (The conditions of housing), Kossuth Könyvkiadó, Budapest.

La Hongrie. L'orientation économique et financière, 1931, Paris, Numero special, Budapest.

Horváth, M., 1980, *Budapest története* (The history of Budapest), Vol. 5, Akadémiai Kiadó, Budapest.

Huszár, T., Léderer, P., 1979, Az értelmiség rekrutációja és funkciói (The recruitment and functions of the intelligentsia), *Társadalmi struktúránk fejlődése* (The development of our social structure), Vol. II, 165–235, Társadalomtudományi Intézet, Budapest.

Illyefalvi, I. L., 1933, *A hatvanéves Budapest* (The sixty-year old Budapest), Budapest Székesfőváros Statisztikai Hivatal, Budapest.

Illyefalvi, I. L., 1935, *A főváros polgári népességének szociális és gazdasági viszonya* (Social and economic conditions of the bourgeois population of the capital), Budapest Székesfőváros Statisztikai Hivatal, Budapest.

Kepecs, J., Klinger, A., 1978, A felsőfokú végzettségűek demográfiai adatai (The demographic data of people of higher education), *Értelmiségiek, diplomások, szellemi munkások* (Intellectuals, graduates, white-collar workers), 261–99, Kossuth Könyvkiadó, Budapest.

Kilényi, G., 1977, *A fővárosi igazgatás és a budapesti agglomerció igazgatásának továbbfejlesztése* (Further development of the public administration of the capital and the Budapest agglomeration), MTA Állam- és Jogtudományi Intézet, Budapest.

Kiss, Gy., 1954, *A budapesti várospolitika 1873–1944* (Urban policy of Budapest 1873–1944), Jogi és Államigazgatási Kiadó, Budapest.

Kolosi, T., 1974, *Társadalmi struktúra és szocializmus* (Social structure and socialism), Kossuth Könyvkiadó, Budapest.

Kolosi, T., 1983, *Struktúra és egyenlőtlenség* (Structure and inequality), Kossuth Könyvkiadó, Budapest.

Kolosi, T., 1984, *Státusz és réteg. Rétegződés vizsgálat III* (Status and stratum. A survey of stratification III), Társadalomtudományi Intézet, Budapest.

Konrád, Gy., Szelényi, I., 1971, A lakáselosztás szociológiai kérdései (Sociological issues of the distribution of flats), *Szocialista városok és a szociológia* (Socialist towns and sociology), 344–68, Kossuth Könyvkiadó, Budapest.

Kőrösi, J., 1870, *Az 1870-dik évbeli pesti népszámlálás eredményei* (The results of the 1870 Census of Pest), Budapest Székesfőváros Statisztikai Hivatalának Közleményei, Budapest.

Kőrösi, J., 1871, *Pest szabad királyi város az 1870-dik évben* (The royal free city of Pest in the year 1870), Budapest Székesfőváros Statisztikai Hivatalának Közleményei, Budapest.

Kőrösi, J., 1876, *Pest város halandósága 1872 s 1873-ban s annak okai* (Mortality in the city of Pest in 1872 and 1873 and its causes), Budapest Székesfőváros Statisztikai Hivatalának Közleményei, Budapest.

Kőrösi, J., 1882, *Budapest nemzetiségi állapota és magyarosodása* (The nationalities of Budapest and its Hungarianization), Az 1881 évi népszámlálás eredményei szerint (According to the results of the 1881 Census), MTA II Osztálya, MTA Könyvkiadó Hivatala, Budapest.

Környezetállapot vizsgálatok (Studies of the condition of the environment), 1990, Fővárosi KJL, Budapest.

Környezetpolitika, alapelvek, célok, eszközök (Environmental policy, principles, objectives, means), 1990, Környezetvédelmi és Vízgazdálkodási Minisztérium, Budapest.

Kósa, J., 1837, *Pest és Buda elmagyarosodása 1848-ig* (Hungarianization of Pest and Buda until 1848), Általános Nyomda, Budapest.

Kovács, Z., Tózsa, I., Gecső, O., 1988, A települési környezet informális rendszere Budapest ökológiai viszonyainak példáján (Informal system of settlement environment. An example of ecological conditions of Budapest), *Városépítés*, Vol. XXIV, No. 5, 16–19.

A lakótelepek főbb adatai. 1980. évi népszámlálás (Major data of housing estates. Census of 1980), 1983, Vol. 35, Központi Statisztikai Hivatal, Budapest.

Lechner, J., 1922, *A régi Pest és Buda* (The Old Pest and Buda), Németh, Élet Nyomda, Budapest.

Lempel, M., 1982, *1800-talsstaden i Budapest dess tillkomst och situation i dag*, Konsthogskolans Arkitekturskola, Stockholm.

Lestyán, S., Sándor, G. Z., 1945, *2000 years old Budapest*, English by Pohárnok, Budapest Székesfőváros Házinyomda, Budapest.

Lukács, J., 1988, *Budapest 1900. A historical portrait of a city and its culture*, Weidenfeld & Nicolson, New York.

Lord, A., 1900, *Budapest a XX. században* (Budapest in the 20th century), Városrendezési tanulmányok, Grill, Budapest.

Markos, Gy., 1971, *Ungarn, Land, Volk, Wirtschaft in Stichworten*, Hirt, Wein.

Márkus, A., 1944, *Adalékok Budapest nagyvárosias kialakulásához 1870–1940 között* (Contributions to the growth of Budapest into a metropolis between 1870 and 1940), Budapest Székesfőváros Házinyomda, Budapest.

Máti, I., 1933, *Budapest környékének közigazgatási rendszere és a nagyvárosi kérdés* (The system of public administration of the vicinity of Budapest and the issue of the metropolis), Csernay Nyomda, Homok.

Mihályi, P., 1983, Történelmi szempontok a magyarországi lakáshiány értékeléséhez (Historical considerations to the assessment of the housing shortage in Hungary), *Lakáspolitikánkról*, 68–83, Kossuth Könyvkiadó, Budapest.

Mónus, L., Mosonyi, T., 1978, *A magyar lakásjog* (The Hungarian law on housing), Közgazdasági és Jogi Könyvkiadó, Budapest.

Móricz, M., 1934, Budapest társadalomrajza (The sociography of Budapest), *Városi Szemle*, Vol. 22, No. 1, 163–232.

Nagy, L., 1959, Rácok Budán és Pesten (1686–1703) (Serbians in Buda and Pest, 1686–

Bibliography

1703), *Tanulmányok Budapest multjából, III* (Studies of the past of Budapest), Akadémiai Kiadó, Budapest.

Nagy, L., 1964, A Viziváros XVII. század végi topográfiája (The topography of Viziváros at the end of the 17th century), *Tanulmányok Budapest múltjából* (Studies of the past of Budapest), XVI, 181–206, Képzőművészeti Alap Kiadó Vállalata, Budapest.

Nagy, L., 1966, Buda polgársága a XVII. század végén (The citizenry of Buda in the late 17th century), *Tanulmányok Budapest multjából* (Studies of the past of Budapest), XVII, 27–59, Múzeumi Ismeretterjesztő Központ, Budapest.

A negyvenéves Budapest. Értekezések a városi közigazgatás köréből (The forty-year-old Budapest. Papers on urban administration), 1914, Jubilee Volume of the *Városi Szemle*.

1949. évi Népszámlálás (The Census of 1949), 1952, Central Statistical Office, Budapest.

1980. évi Népszámlálás (The Census of 1980), 1981, Central Statistical Office, Budapest.

Ongjert, R., Nagy, T., 1989, *A lakásépítés finanszírozási és támogatási konstrukciójának nemzetközi összehasonlítása* (International comparison of the construction of financing and subsidies of housing), Budapesti Városépítési Tervező Vállalat, Budapest.

Országh, S., 1885, *Budapest középítkezései 1868–1882* (Public building activities of Budapest between 1868 and 1882), Nagel B., Budapest.

Országos Környezetvédelmi Koncepció és Követelményrendszer (National concept and norms of environmental protection), 1980, Országos Környezet-és Természetvédelmi Hivatal, Budapest.

Palugyai, I., 1852, *Buda-Pest szabad királyi városok leírása* (The description of the royal free cities of Buda and Pest), Landerer and Heckenast, Pest.

Pécsi, M. (ed.), 1959, *Budapest természeti földrajza* (Physical geography of Budapest), Akadémiai Kiadó, Budapest.

Perczel, K., 1989, A magyarországi regionális tervezés történetéhez (On the history of Hungarian regional planning), *Tér és társadalom*, Vol. 3, No. 3, 81–106.

Pető, I., Szakács, S., 1985, *A hazai gazdaság négy évtizedének története 1945–1985. Az ujjáépítés és a terv utasításos irányítás időszaka* (The history of the four decades of the domestic economy between 1945 and 1985. The period of reconstruction and 'commanded' system), Vol. I, Közgazdasági és Jogi Könyvkiadó, Budapest.

Petrik, A., 1909. *A régi Budapest építőművészete* (The architecture of the old Budapest), Vols. 1–4, Nagel B., Budapest.

Pikler, J. Gy., 1917, Halandóság és szociális tagozódás Budapesten (Mortality and social stratification in Budapest), *Huszadik század*, Vol. 18, No. 36, 310–17.

Preisich, G., 1960, *Budapest városépítésének története Buda visszavételétől a kiegyezésig* (The history of urban architecture of Budapest from the Reconquest of Buda until the Compromise), Műszaki Könyvkiadó, Budapest.

Preisich, G., 1964, *Budapest városépítészetének története a kiegyezéstől a Tanácsköztársaságig* (The history of urban architecture of Budapest from the Compromise until the Republic of Councils), Műszaki Könyvkiadó, Budapest.

Preisich, G. (ed.), 1973, *Budapest jövője* (The future of Budapest), Műszaki Könyvkiadó, Budapest.

Preisich, G. (ed.), 1973, *Budapest városrendezési problémái* (Urban planning problems of Budapest), Mimeo Felsőktatási Jegyzetellátó, Budapest.

Preisich, G., 1979, Entwicklungs- und Plannungsprobleme der stadt Budapest. *Mitteilungen der Österreichischen Geographischen Gesellschaft*, Vol. 121, No. 1, 7–128.

Probáld, F., 1974, *Budapest városklímája* (Urban climate of Budapest), Akadémiai Kiadó, Budapest.

Radisics, E., 1932, *Hungary Yesterday and Today*, Richards, London.

Rados, J., 1928, *Budapest városépítészetének története* (The history of urban architecture of Budapest), Böm Nyomda, Budapest.

Ságvári, Á., 1973, *Budapest. The history of a capital*, Corvina, Budapest.

Bibliography

Sándor, P., 1983, A fővárosi lakásépítés hatékonysága (Efficiency of housing in the capital), *Lakáspolitikánk*, 250–61, Kossuth Könyvkiadó, Budapest.

Siklóssy, L., 1931, *Hogyan épült Budapest (1870–1930)* (How Budapest was built between 1870 and 1930), The Committee of Public Works, Budapest.

Sillince, J. A. A., 1985, The housing market of the Budapest urban region 1949–1963, *Urban Studies*, Vol. 22, No. 1, 1–9.

Spira, Gy., Vörös, K., 1978, *Budapest története* (The history of Budapest), Akadémiai Kiadó, Budapest.

Szelényi, I., Konrád, Gy., 1969, *Az új lakótelepek szociológiai problémái* (Sociological problems of the new housing estates), Akadémiai Kiadó, Budapest.

Szelényi, I., 1972, *Társadalmi struktúra és lakásrendszer* (Social structure and housing system), Ph.D. dissertation, Budapest.

Szelényi, I., 1974, Urbanizáció és az életmód alakulása Budapesten (Urbanization and changes in the lifestyle of Budapest), *Tanulmányok Budapest múltjából XX*, 229–43, Budapesti Történeti Múzeum évkönyve, Budapest.

Szelényi, I., 1976, Gestion regionale et classe sociale. Le cas de l'Europe de l'Est, *Revue française de Sociologie*, Vol. XVII, Nr. 1. Jan.–March.

Szelényi, I., 1990, *Új osztály, állam, politika* (New class, state, politics), Európa Könyvkiadó, Budapest.

Szigeti, J., 1933, *Budapest (Buda, Óbuda s Pest) a XIX. század első harmadában* (Budapest/Buda, Old Buda, and Pest/ in the first decades of the 19th century), Egyetemi Nyomda, Budapest.

Szirmai, V., 1989, *A környezetvédelem érdekviszonyai és a környezetvédelmi politika* (Interest relationships and policy of environmental protection), Summary of a research project, Ministry of Environmental Protection and Water Management, Budapest.

Szviezsényi, Z., 1939, *Budapest, ville d'eaux*, ed. par le Comité Centrales des Stations Thermales et Climatiques de Budapest, Pallas, Budapest.

Tábori, P., 1939, *The real Hungary, III*, Skeffington & Son, London.

Thirring, G., 1935, *Budapest főváros demográfiai és társadalmi tagozódásának a fejlődése az utolsó ötven évben* (The development of demographic and social statification of Budapest during the last fifty years), Vols. 1–2, Budapest Székesfőváros Statisztikai Hivatal, Budapest.

Vági, G., 1962, *Versengés a fejlesztési forrásokért. Területi elosztás – társadalmi egyenlőtlenségek* (Competition for the development resources. Territorial distribution – social inequalities), Közgazdasági és Jogi Könyvkiadó, Budapest.

Várnai, S., 1905, Adalékok a régi pesti polgári rend társadalmi, gazdasági kialakulásához. Pest város társadalmi, gazdasági élete a 17–18. században (Contributions to the social and economic evolution of the old estate of burghers of Pest. Social and economic life of Pest in the 17th and 18th centuries), *Magyar Gazdaság, Történelmi Szemle*, Vol. 12, Nos. 3–4, 241–57.

Völgyes, I., 1982, *Hungary. A Nation of Contradictions*, Westview, Boulder, Col.

Zoltán, J., 1963, *A barokk Pest-Buda élete. Ünnepségek, szórakozások, szokások* (The life of the Baroque Pest and Buda. Festivals, entertainment, customs), Fővárosi Szabó Ervin Könyvtár, Budapest.

Index

Index

Index